WRECKS AND RESCUES OF THE GREAT LAKES

WRECKS AND RESCUES OF THE GREAT LAKES

A PHOTOGRAPHIC HISTORY

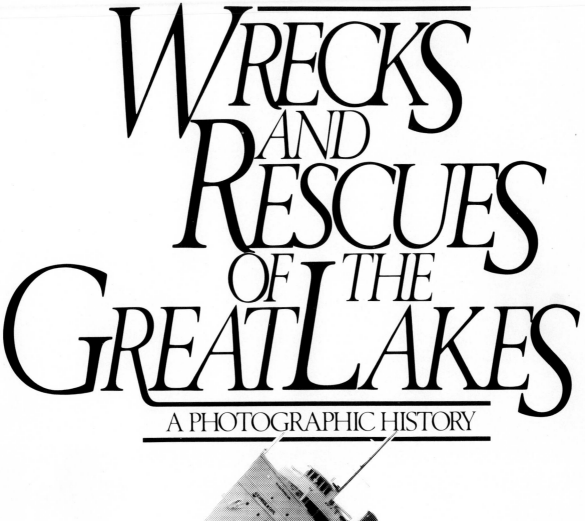

JAMES P. BARRY

San Diego   a Howell -North book   California

First Edition
Manufactured in the United States of America

For information write to:
Howell-North Books
P.O. Box 3051
La Jolla, California 92038

Library of Congress Cataloging in Publication Data

The part of this book dealing with the wreck of the steamer
Monarch is reprinted by permission from *Inland Seas*®, quarterly journal of the Great Lakes Historical Society, Spring
1980.

1 2 3 4 5 6 7 8 9   84 83 82 81

Opposite: The steamer *Pilgrim* aground four
miles south of Lakeview, Michigan, on Lake
Huron, April 29, 1907. She was pounded to
pieces where she lay. (From the Collections of the
Michigan History Division)

WRECKS AND RESCUES OF THE GREAT LAKES

A PHOTOGRAPHIC HISTORY

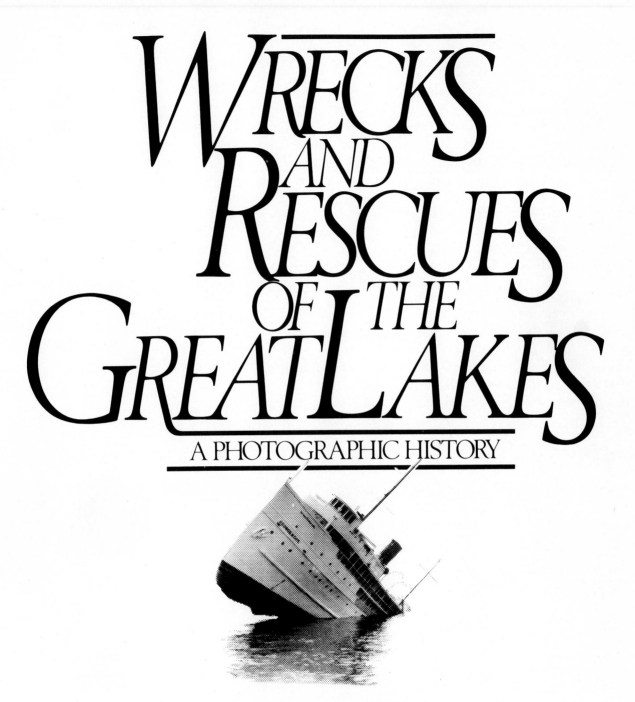

JAMES P. BARRY

San Diego · a Howell-North book · California

First Edition
Manufactured in the United States of America

For information write to:
Howell-North Books
P.O. Box 3051
La Jolla, California 92038

Library of Congress Cataloging in Publication Data

The part of this book dealing with the wreck of the steamer *Monarch* is reprinted by permission from *Inland Seas*®, quarterly journal of the Great Lakes Historical Society, Spring 1980.

1 2 3 4 5 6 7 8 9   84 83 82 81

Opposite: The steamer *Pilgrim* aground four miles south of Lakeview, Michigan, on Lake Huron, April 29, 1907. She was pounded to pieces where she lay. (From the Collections of the Michigan History Division)

For
E.P.H.
Who suggested this book

*They know what shipwrecks are, for out of sight of land,
however inland, they have drowned full many a midnight ship
with all its shrieking crew.*
— Herman Melville, describing the Great Lakes in
Moby Dick.

Contents

Acknowledgments

or help in gathering photographs and information about wrecks, I am indebted to many more people than can be listed. Particular thanks must go to the Rev. Edward J. Dowling, S.J., dean of Great Lakes historians; J. Leo Finn; Patrick Folkes; Skip Gillham; Robert Graham; Edith Gvora, Thunder Bay Public Library; Janice L. Haas, Rutherford B. Hayes Library; Robert E. Lee and M. Jackson of the Dossin Great Lakes Museum; Robert MacDonald; Daniel C. McCormick; Paul A. Michaels; Arthur N. O'Hara, Great Lakes Historical Society; Richard F. Palmer; Patrick M. Quinn, University Archivist, Northwestern University; Ruth Revels, Marine Room, Milwaukee Public Library; Janet Coe Sanborn, editor, *Inland Seas*; Kenneth Thro; Richard J. Wright and Gary L. Bailey of the Center for Archival Collections, Bowling Green State University; and the helpful people in the Marine Investigation Division of the U.S. Coast Guard, the Public Archives of Canada, and the U.S. National Archives.

The three-masted schooner *T. R. Merritt* aground on the southern shore of Lake Ontario, five miles east of Fair Haven light. She ran aground on the morning of September 12, 1900, in a storm that caused at least one other wreck. She seems permanently ashore here, but she was later pulled off and she lasted another 16 years. (Courtesy Dossin Great Lakes Museum)

Acknowledgments

For help in gathering photographs and information about wrecks, I am indebted to many more people than can be listed. Particular thanks must go to the Rev. Edward J. Dowling, S.J., dean of Great Lakes historians; J. Leo Finn; Patrick Folkes; Skip Gillham; Robert Graham; Edith Gvora, Thunder Bay Public Library; Janice L. Haas, Rutherford B. Hayes Library; Robert E. Lee and M. Jackson of the Dossin Great Lakes Museum; Robert MacDonald; Daniel C. McCormick; Paul A. Michaels; Arthur N. O'Hara, Great Lakes Historical Society; Richard F. Palmer; Patrick M. Quinn, University Archivist, Northwestern University; Ruth Revels, Marine Room, Milwaukee Public Library; Janet Coe Sanborn, editor, *Inland Seas*; Kenneth Thro; Richard J. Wright and Gary L. Bailey of the Center for Archival Collections, Bowling Green State University; and the helpful people in the Marine Investigation Division of the U.S. Coast Guard, the Public Archives of Canada, and the U.S. National Archives.

The three-masted schooner *T. R. Merritt* aground on the southern shore of Lake Ontario, five miles east of Fair Haven light. She ran aground on the morning of September 12, 1900, in a storm that caused at least one other wreck. She seems permanently ashore here, but she was later pulled off and she lasted another 16 years. (Courtesy Dossin Great Lakes Museum)

W.A.W. Catinus, Chief, Marine Casualty Investigations, Transport Canada; Capt. R. L. Davis, Hall Corporation; M. Fraleigh, Sarnia Public Library; Alan Howard, Marine Museum of Upper Canada; Ruth M. Kirkland, Hackley Public Library, Muskegon; G. Noble, Thunder Bay Historical Society; T. Michael O'Brien, U.S.C.G.; Robert D. Patterson, Michigan Technical University Library; Linda Penstone-Parsley, Toronto Harbour Commissioners; Ralph K. Roberts; Alfred E. Sagon-King; Capt. Robert A. Sinclair; Susan Soboslai, Great Lakes Historical Society; Margaret Van Every, Archives of Ontario; Lt. Charles T. Winfrey, U.S.C.G.

Bayfield, Wisconsin, Public Library; Chicago Historical Society; Cleveland Public Library; Collingwood Museum; Duluth Public Library; Library of Congress; Mariners Museum; Metropolitan Toronto Public Libraries; Michigan History Division; *Milwaukee Journal*; Ninth District, U.S. Coast Guard; *St. Catherine's Standard*; State Historical Society of Wisconsin; University of Western Ontario Library; Western Reserve Historical Society, Cleveland.

Acknowledgment should also be made of those who have written about the Lakes, either in books or in the pages of *Inland Seas, Telescope,* and other journals. Among them are the late Dana T. Bowen, the late Dwight Boyer, Alexander C. Meaken, T. Michael O'Brien, and Dr. Julius F. Wolff, Jr. The specific ways in which I have drawn on their work are explained in the Bibliography and Notes.

Particular thanks go to my wife, Anne, who helped in every way from guarding against interruptions to proofreading.

The *L. C. Smith* ashore on Lake Superior, just east of Two Harbors, Minnesota, after attempting to enter harbor in fog on July 9, 1910, navigating by dead reckoning and using only the fog signal for bearings. She was duly refloated and repaired, and she sailed again. (Courtesy K. E. Thro)

1

Introduction

The Canadian sidewheeler *Rothesay* was carrying excursionists on the upper St. Lawrence on the night of September 12, 1889, when she collided with the tug *Myra*. Two of the crew of the tug were killed. The *Rothesay* was beached near Prescott, Ontario, and all aboard got off safely. The steamer was a total loss. (Courtesy Richard J. Wright Great Lakes Marine Collection)

Shipwrecks began on the Great Lakes of North America almost as soon as there were ships to be wrecked. One of the first vessels that the French built—on Lake Ontario in 1678—the little 10-ton *Frontenac*, was lost in a wreck a year later.

An early British wreck on the Lakes was that of the *Ontario*, a 16-gun snow that was launched on Lake Ontario in the spring of 1780. The *Ontario* was the largest vessel then sailing the Lakes; she was 77 feet long on deck and measured 231 tons. Leaving Niagara on October 31, 1780, she encountered a violent gale that blew all that night and the next day. Afterward some of her gratings, her binnacle, oars from her boats, some of her seamen's hats, part of her quarter gallery, and other debris washed ashore, but nothing more was ever seen of her, or of the 40 seamen, 30 soldiers and 4 officers who were aboard.

Marine photography did not appear until the 1850s. Cameras of that day were bulky wooden boxes mounted on large, heavy tripods, and they often had to be accompanied by portable darkrooms. Little wonder that at first they were not carried about freely, and that when they were turned toward marine subjects they usually were set up overlooking sunny harbors, where they could take pictures of ships from static vantage points.

This equipment was scarcely suited for making pictures of wrecks. Problems met by a photographer who had to travel quickly with such clumsy gear to the scene of a disaster by horse-drawn vehicle or boat were nearly insurmountable. But cameras became easier to use and slightly easier to carry. By 1885, pictures of the isolated wreck of the Canadian Pacific steamer *Algoma* were taken by an energetic photographer who traveled to the scene by tugboat.

Within the next few years photography became more common, and more photographers set up shops in towns and cities around the Lakes. When a wreck occurred, there was a growing possibility that a photographer would be on hand to respond to it, and as the nineteenth century moved into the twentieth, more pictures of wrecks were taken. Even so, only a tiny percentage was ever photographed, and undoubtedly some of the photos that were made have since disappeared. A collection such as the one in this book shows, at best, a small part of the disasters that actually happened.

*S*ince navigation began on the Lakes there have been, it is estimated, some 10,000 wrecks there—about the same quantity as have happened around the British Isles in the past 300 years. As large numbers of ships have operated on the Lakes only in the last century and a half, and as the British Isles were long the maritime center of the world, the comparison is striking.

Lake navigation is difficult. Sea room is limited on the Great Lakes, and whichever way the wind blows, a vessel is usually on a lee shore. Natural harbors are scarce and manmade harbors difficult to enter in a storm. Fog is common. Ships operate not only in open water, but also through the narrow channels and rivers that connect the Lakes; such passages as the Straits of Mackinac and the reef-strewn entrance to Georgian Bay are notorious graveyards of ships. Winter ice adds complications.

The freighter *E. C. Pope* striking a pier at the entrance to Duluth harbor as she runs for shelter during the storm of November 28, 1905. She reached harbor with only minor damage. (Courtesy K. E. Thro)

The reef- and island-strewn passage between Lake Huron and Georgian Bay was the scene of many wrecks. The *Forest City*, running at full steam through dense fog, slammed into Bear's Rump Island on June 5, 1904. She stuck so firmly that she defied all attempts to salvage her, but as water seeped into the hull through her damaged bow, she filled, and the weight of the water caused her to slide off and sink in deep water. (Courtesy Patrick Folkes)

The *Howard M. Hanna, Jr.*, one of the ships wrecked in the "Big Blow" of November 1913, shown here in happier circumstances. (Mariners Museum, Newport News, Va.)

Ships have been lost on the Lakes in nearly every year and from nearly every cause, but occasionally these waters have been wracked by storms so great, with losses so extreme, that they are major events in history. Such an event was the "Big Blow" of November 1913 in which 19 ships were stranded, 6 were driven ashore as total losses and 12 others vanished completely. Between 250 and 300 people died. On Lake Huron, near the small Canadian town of Goderich alone, the bodies of 25 drowned or frozen seamen were washed ashore. Twenty-two others came ashore near Thedford, another town on the Canadian side of that lake.

Storms that sweep the Lakes may begin as low-pressure areas over many parts of the North American continent—most often, perhaps, northwestern Canada, the Gulf Coast or the Rocky Mountains. The great storm of 1913 began in all three of these regions; it was actually three storms, growing, moving faster and colliding over the Great Lakes. But these storm patterns are by no means invariable. In November 1905, a storm, small only by comparison with the 1913 storm, swept in unexpectedly from the northeast over Lake Superior on the very heels of another storm and caught ships emerging from shelter and going about their business. It left 19 of them total losses and at least 78 seamen dead.

The power of a storm can seem unlimited. Captain Hagen of the 500-foot-long *Howard M. Hanna, Jr.*, which was wrecked on Lake Huron in the 1913 storm, related that the waves "carried away the after cabin, broke in the windows and doors of the pilot house and tore off its top." No matter how he tried to control her, his ship fell off into the trough of the sea and "commenced to roll and tumble, and the mountainous seas smashed over her." Tons of icy water dropped onto her decks, then poured into the engine room through broken doors

Above: During the 1913 storm, bodies of seamen were washed ashore at many places around the Lakes. Twenty-five came ashore near Goderich, Ontario, alone. Here the funeral procession for five unidentified sailors rounds the central town park in Goderich. (Courtesy Captain Robert A. Sinclair)

Left: Floating upside down in Lake Huron after the storm of November 13, 1913, this "mystery ship" was finally identified a week later by a diver as the *Charles S. Price*, a 524-foot steel steamer with a cargo of coal. All 28 people aboard perished. The derelict sank not long after the diver identified it. (Courtesy Hamilton Collection, Rutherford B. Hayes Library)

Ice has also made Great Lakes navigation difficult. The steamer *Pere Marquette 3* was caught in a Lake Michigan ice pack in March 1920. Her passengers and crew were able to walk across the ice to a nearby steel car ferry, but the wooden hull of the vessel was crushed by ice and her upper works were sheared off. (Courtesy Marine Historical Collection, Milwaukee Public Library)

Ice conditions on the wreck of the steel steamer *Agawa*, which struck Advance Reef, Lake Huron, in December 1927. (Courtesy Collingwood Museum)

and damaged cabins, but the men worked on knee-deep in it to keep the engines turning. Despite her laboring engines, she was gradually driven near shore and "in a very short time the great waves rode her to destruction. She drifted broadside onto the reef at 10:00 P.M. The port side fetched up on the rocks first and the seas and wind pounded her the rest of the way onto the reef." Later the captain saw "that the vessel was broken in two about the after side of number seven hatch. You could see the wide crack across the deck and down the side. The smoke stack was gone, and the life rafts and starboard lifeboat had been carried away. . . ." It is not hard to imagine what happened to the vessels that were swallowed up completely in the storm, among them two ocean freighters and a lightship.

Such disasters may seem to be comfortably past, but even now—with better equipment and bigger ships—there are losses, though not on such a vast scale. In November—that haunted month—of 1975 the 729-foot-long steel ore carrier *Edmund Fitzgerald* disappeared at night in a Lake Superior storm, going down so quickly that the men aboard could not

even send a radio message. The master of another freighter nearby reported that suddenly he lost sight of the running lights of the ship and that "the next thing we knew they were off the radar screen." The ship and her crew of 29 simply vanished. There remained only the traditional service in the old Mariners' Church at Detroit, where a clergyman said prayers for the seamen and the church bell tolled 29 times.

There have also been wrecks that happened quietly, when the Lakes were in a different mood. Some were tragicomic episodes. Consider the passenger ship *George M. Cox*, freshly painted white, her crew in high holiday spirits, on her way to Port Arthur in May 1933 to pick up Canadian excursionists and carry them to the Chicago World's Fair. Steaming across Lake Superior in a low-lying fog, she followed a course that would take her past the southwestern tip of Isle Royale. Off that end of the big island stands a lighthouse marking a notable hazard to navigation called "Rock of Ages." High in the tower of the lighthouse, about 6:00 P.M., Lightkeeper John Soldenski was at work. He could see over the fog layer and he watched as two masts of a ship moved briskly past his location while the ship herself was hidden. Then, the two masts slowly turned and headed directly for him. The keeper repeatedly blew his foghorn, but to no avail. Traveling at about 18 knots, the *Cox* ran straight up on the reef. Luckily the sea was calm and all 120 people aboard were easily ferried to safety by the ship and lighthouse keeper's boats. They merely spent a sober, miserable night shivering in the cold and taking turns warming themselves in the lighthouse, which did not have room for all of them at one time.

To help mariners in distress, the United States Government in 1875 and 1876 established on the Great Lakes 29 lifesaving stations. They were part of a federal system on both the Atlantic Coast and the Lakes that in 1878 was formally organized as the U.S. Life Saving Service. The crews on the Lakes soon began to wear a uniform, which in 1889 was adopted throughout the service. By 1900 there were 60 stations on the Great Lakes. In 1915 they became part of the U.S. Coast Guard. Between 1882 and 1889 the Canadian Government set up 10 lifesaving stations on the Lakes and still others on the Atlantic. As years passed, a few more Canadian stations were established.

Possibly the most unusual station of the United States Life Saving Service was located on the Great Lakes, at Northwestern University in Evanston, Illinois. Its beginnings antedated most other stations. The many wrecks on Lake Michigan in the 1850s, culminating in that of the passenger steamer *Lady Elgin* in

Having run at speed onto Rock of Ages reef, Lake Superior, in a fog, the *George M. Cox* lies poised with her bow in the air while her stern is awash. All aboard were saved; the ship later broke up and sank. (Courtesy Richard J. Wright Great Lakes Marine Collection; and Center for Archival Collections, Bowling Green State University)

1860, brought demands that lifeboat stations be set up along the western shore of the lake. A Northwestern student, Edward Spencer—helped by some of his classmates—had managed to pull 17 of the *Lady Elgin's* passengers from the gray waves on that occasion. In a somewhat belated gesture, in 1871 the U.S. Navy offered a lifeboat to the university with the proviso that the institution train for it a crew from the student body. The offer was accepted and the crew was provided, although no rescues are recorded in the early years of the project. When lifesaving stations were officially formed, the small building of the earliest first-grade station on the Lakes, the Evanston Station, was erected in 1876 on the Northwestern University campus. Students continued to make up the crew, though the keeper (the man in charge of the station, usually termed "captain") became a full-time professional; for many years he was Captain Lawrence O. Lawson.

The Evanston crew functioned well on such occasions as the wreck of the schooner *Jamaica* in 1885, when they took off all hands by breeches buoy, and the wreck of the steamer *Calumet* on Thanksgiving Day 1889, when they rescued her crew of 18 by making three trips with a surfboat through a fierce Lake Michigan blizzard. "The flying spray from every wave-crest left a glaze of ice on every object it struck, the men's clothing being covered, while the oars were constantly slipping from the rowlocks, the latter as well as the oars being so encased with it." This action won each of the lifesavers the gold medal of the U.S. Life Saving Service—its highest award. Students continued to man the station, in later years under Captain Peter Jensen, until the Coastguardsmen took over in 1916. From 1876 to 1916 the Evanston crew saved over 400 lives.

The earliest test of a motorized lifeboat anywhere in the service was carried out on the Lakes by Keeper Henry J.

The Evanston, Illinois, lifesaving crew launching a surfboat. This crew was unique; all but the captain were students at Northwestern University. (Chicago Historical Society)

The Grand Marais, Michigan, lifesaving crew in their surfboat, with Captain Trudell at the steering oar. The surfboat was lighter and more maneuverable than the lifeboat, and the lifesavers usually preferred to use it when they could. (From the Collections of the Michigan History Division)

A wreck about to happen. As the schooner *Len Higby* drags ashore in Lake Michigan off Frankfort on October 30, 1898, lifesavers rescue the crew. (From the Collections of the Michigan History Division)

Lifesaving crew going out to the wreck of the *Francis Hinton*, Two Rivers, Wisconsin, November 16, 1909. (Courtesy Ninth District, U.S. Coast Guard)

Bringing a surfboat ashore at Ludington, Michigan. (Courtesy Ninth District, U.S. Coast Guard)

Canadian lifesaving crew and lifeboat at Point Traverse, Lake Ontario, taken between 1883 and 1900. Lifeboats often were carried in this way to a point on shore near a wreck. (Courtesy Public Archives of Canada C 45419)

Canadian lifeboat crew at Collingwood, on Georgian Bay. The crew evidently dressed up to have their pictures taken. Note the difference between the lifeboat, shown here, and the surfboat. The lifeboat was more heavily built, had enclosed ends and usually steered with a rudder. It was sturdier than the surfboat but less maneuverable. (Courtesy Collingwood Museum)

Left: When *Pere Marquette 3* ran aground in a January storm off Ludington, Michigan, in 1903, those aboard were brought ashore over the ice-filled water of Lake Michigan by breeches buoy. (Courtesy Great Lakes Historical Society)

Right: The steamer *Argo*, bound from Chicago to Holland, Michigan, arrived off Holland on November 24, 1906, in a fierce gale. Attempting to enter harbor, she was dashed against the pierheads by heavy seas and then carried to a sandbar about 500 feet from shore. The lifesavers brought the 19 passengers ashore by breeches buoy; the crew members stayed on board and were taken off later. The steamer remained there through the winter and was pulled off the next spring. (Courtesy Rev. Edward J. Dowling, S.J.)

Cleary of the Marquette, Michigan station. The first motor lifeboat was the result of a collaboration between Cleary, Lieutenant C. H. McLellan of the Revenue Cutter Service, a man of some experience with lifeboats (revenue cutters had long had a secondary role as rescue vessels), and the Lake Shore Engine Works which manufactured internal combustion engines. The boat was launched in September 1899. Trials by Cleary in Lake Superior storms were successful enough that a commission headed by Professor C. H. Peabody of the Massachusetts Institute of Technology was appointed to study the matter; in due course they recommended conversion by the Life Saving Service to power lifeboats. By the end of 1905, 12 of them were in operation throughout the service.

Men of the Life Saving Service were folk heroes of their day; they routinely risked their lives to save others. One of the stations was at Cleveland. A wreck there on November 11, 1883, was of a kind that happened often on the Lakes because they lack sea room and natural shelters: a vessel running for a manmade harbor missed the entrance. At half past seven in the evening, "suddenly and without a moment's warning," the wind hauled to the northwest and began to blow. About 9:00 P.M. the schooner barge *John T. Johnson* approached the harbor under mainsail and forestaysail, her foreboom having carried away. She missed the entrance and dropped anchor off a pier to the east of the breakwater, but as she paid out anchor chain she drifted to a dangerous position inside the end of the pier. The lifesaving crew, having been assured by a tugboat captain that if they boarded the schooner and passed him a line he would pull her off, manned the surfboat and pulled out of the harbor into the heavy seas—so heavy that from the men's viewpoint the waves completely blanketed the light that should have shone through the darkness

Left: U.S. Life Saving Station at Evanston, Illinois, on the Northwestern University campus, in the 1880s. (Courtesy Northwestern University Archives)

Right: The station at Evanston, 1890-91. The left wing has been added. (Courtesy Northwestern University Archives)

from the end of the pier. Keeping the bow of the surfboat to the storm, the oarsmen backed down toward the schooner, came alongside and boarded her. "The sea was making a clean breach over her at the time and the water froze as fast as it struck," Keeper Goodwin later reported. They were so close to land that Goodwin could call to men ashore to send out the tug; but by that time not one of the tugs in the harbor was willing to risk the attempt.

Goodwin decided that taking the *Johnson's* crew ashore by boat was too dangerous and that he would have to land again and get them off by breeches buoy. Leaving one of his men aboard the vessel, he pulled away in the surfboat toward the harbor entrance. As the oars dug into the waves, a heavy sea broke over the boat and half filled it. Goodwin saw then that he could not reach the shelter of the harbor breakwater, but instead must beach the boat. The one beach available was only 150 feet wide and was situated between two piers. As the crew approached it, their boat suddenly broached to and capsized, throwing the men into the icy water. Struggling, they were carried shoreward by the waves, buried in the breakers and pulled back by the undertow over and over again. An excited crowd had gathered on one pier. Think-

ing to help, some of them threw planks and timbers into the water; these objects immediately became wave-driven battering rams that the men had to avoid at all costs. Then someone on the pier threw lines to the men and pulled three of them out. The others clung to the overturned boat until it drifted to a place where ready hands on shore could reach it and drag it to land.

The crew, "now more dead than alive," were taken to the nearby customs house and given dry clothing. No sooner had they changed than a man came in to report that the vessel was breaking up. The lifesavers hurried to their station "as fast as they were able in the circumstances," got the necessary rescue equipment and returned to the beach. The ship's crew by this time had climbed well up in the rigging, for not only was the deck crusted with ice from breaking waves, but so was the rigging to a height of 15 feet above it. At five minutes after midnight, using the Lyle gun, the

The Life Saving Station at Charlevoix, on
northern Lake Michigan, in 1908. (Courtesy
Library of Congress)

Beach apparatus drill by the Charlevoix lifesaving
crew, 1908. The beach cart carried their gear; the
Lyle gun at lower left was used to shoot lines
aboard wrecked vessels; and the floating object at
left is the life car, an enclosed capsule used to
bring people ashore through high seas and surf.
(Courtesy Library of Congress)

lifesavers shot a line into the mizzen crosstrees and the lifesaver who had stayed on the schooner secured it. They brought the woman cook ashore in the breeches buoy and by 12:55 the *Johnson's* whole crew of six men and one woman were ashore.

Not all rescues were successful. The grim joke that the lifesavers had to go out, but they didn't have to come back, was true enough. On one occasion the crew at Point aux Barques on Lake Huron set out in a heavy storm to reach a vessel that had struck unusually far offshore. Their boat capsized twice and they righted it. Then it capsized again and rolled over, capsizing and righting itself several times in the waves as the men clung to it until they fell away, one by one. In time the boat, with only Keeper Jerome G. Kiah still alive, was washed ashore. He was found on the beach, tottering and dazed, muttering, "Poor boys! Poor boys! They are all gone—all gone."

Evanston (Northwestern University) lifesaving crew launching a surfboat, c. 1909. (Courtesy Northwestern University Archives)

Most shipping disasters have taken place outside the view of cameras, the commonest of them being the final moments of those many ships that have simply "sailed away," as lake sailors say of vessels that never reach port again.

One such vessel was the side-wheel steamer *Waubuno*. On Georgian Bay in the late 1870s, the *Waubuno* under Captain George Burkett competed with the newer *Magnettawan* under Captain John O'Donnell. They carried passengers and freight from the towns at the southern end of the Bay to settlements scattered along the North Shore and the North Channel. The largest of these was Parry Sound.

By late November 1879 there had been several storms on the Lakes. The two steamers lay at the dock in Collingwood, waiting to carry an assortment of freight and a number of passengers to Parry Sound and points beyond, while a

By the 1920s motor lifeboats had come into use. The Coast Guard crew at Ludington. (Courtesy Marine Historical Collection, Milwaukee Public Library)

The *J. R. Sensibar* grounded on July 9, 1941, and Coast Guardsmen performed the traditional lifesaving duties, shooting a line aboard and rigging a breeches buoy. (Courtesy Hamilton Collection, Rutherford B. Hayes Library; from the Collections of the Michigan History Division)

fall gale raged outside the harbor. The *Waubuno's* cargo was overdue on the North Shore and her crew and passengers were beginning to grumble at the delay. Some of the *Waubuno's* passengers slept on board; others stayed at hotels in town. Among those who slept on board were a young doctor and his wife. He was setting out to begin practice in one of the small northern villages. That night the doctor's wife had a terrible nightmare, in which the *Waubuno* was wrecked and everyone on board was lost. Next morning she told it at breakfast, and soon everyone on board and a good many people on shore knew about it. Despite the young woman's misgivings, the couple stayed on board—their belongings had been stowed in the hold and their tickets purchased.

The following night the *Waubuno* still lay at the dock as snow squalls whipped the harbor. Then, at 3:30 in the morning, Captain Burkett decided he

would sail at 4:00. A messenger went running to one of the hotels to rout out the passengers asleep there. Not many responded, and a few of the slower ones arrived angrily at the dock to see the lights of the boat disappearing into the windy darkness. Those same lights were seen a bit later by Lighthouse Keeper John Hoar at Christian Island as the *Waubuno* passed.

At 10:00 that morning the *Magnettawan* started out, but Captain O'Donnell soon concluded that the storm was too great and went into shelter behind Christian Island; there he lay for

One of the most common kinds of disaster on the Lakes occurred when a vessel running for shelter in a storm missed a harbor entrance. About 1885 an unidentified schooner was wrecked against the harbor pier at Manitowoc, Wisconsin, having missed the harbor entrance. Flying spray obscures the lower left corner of the picture. (State Historical Society of Wisconsin)

Having missed the entrance to the harbor at Frankfort on Lake Michigan on October 4, 1897, the little schooner *Addie* was washed sideways onto the beach, becoming a total loss. Here her crew removes the scant belongings and furniture. (Courtesy Rev. Edward J. Dowling, S.J.)

40 hours while the gale grew wilder, then slowly blew itself out. Three days after the two steamers left Collingwood, the *Magnettawan* came into harbor at Parry Sound. There was no sign of the *Waubuno*.

At first everyone supposed that she was still in shelter along the way or that she had run aground. A lumber tug was sent out to find her. What the tug found was wreckage strewn along the rocks and islands just below Copperhead. Loggers who had been working at Moon River, near Copperhead, reported that in the middle of a heavy snow storm, near noon that day, they had heard a steamer whistling in distress. All of the life jackets of the *Waubuno* were eventually recovered unused, but none of the bodies of the 24 people aboard, including the doctor and his wife, were ever found. The fol-lowing March an Indian found the hull upside down on the shore of what now is called Wreck Island, just north of Moose Point. The cabins and machinery had disappeared.

No one knows just what happened to her. A few years ago her anchor was discovered on the bottom by scuba divers and since then a theory has been suggested. It seems likely that she tried to enter her usual approach to Parry Sound, the narrow channel known as Waubuno Channel, that she was blinded by the snow storm and that she turned back to go through the gap at Copperhead. Unable to find it in the storm, Captain Burkett dropped anchor, but in the storm the anchor dragged. During this time the little ship began her whistles of distress. As the anchor continued to drag, she slid downwind to a shoal where the waves picked her up, turned her over, and smashed her down so hard that the main engine was dashed through the side of the hull and the hull split in two lengthwise. Her upper works, carrying the bodies of all on board, drifted off downwind to sink in deep water.

Opposite top: Lifesavers take the crew off the three-master *J. A. Holmes* at an unidentified time and place. The schooner survived this incident, for she eventually went to salt water and was lost there in 1917. (Courtesy Marine Historical Collection, Milwaukee Public Library)

Opposite bottom: The three-master *Emily B. Maxwell* missed the harbor entrance at Cleveland and piled up against the breakwater in a Lake Erie storm, on August 31, 1909. She was a total loss. (Courtesy Hamilton Collection, Rutherford B. Hayes Library)

Above: Ashore at Oswego, New York, the *Albacore* is pounded by Lake Ontario breakers. Running before a 40-mile-per-hour wind, she approached Oswego harbor at 7:30 in the morning of September 12, 1900. A harbor tug took a line from her, but the wind was so strong that the schooner pulled the small tug toward shore. Finally the crew of the tug had to cut the cable and head for deeper water, leaving the *Albacore* to her fate. Those aboard got ashore safely, but the schooner was abandoned where she lay. (Courtesy J. Leo Finn)

Not all vessels that "sailed away" left harbor in stormy weather. The year after the *Waubuno* was lost, the sidewheeler *Alpena* steamed out of Grand Haven, Michigan, on a warm, delightful Friday evening, the 15th of October, bound for Chicago. In the middle of Lake Michigan, about 1:00 A.M., she met and passed the steamer *Muskegon*, exchanging the normal whistle salutes. Shortly afterward the weather changed swiftly; the thermometer dropped 33 degrees in an hour, tornado-strength winds swept over the lake, and the snow became blinding. Altogether in that storm—which since has come to be known as "the *Alpena* Storm"—94 vessels were wrecked or damaged and 118 lives were lost. The *Alpena* and the 80 or more people aboard were never seen again, though some of her debris was found floating off Holland, Michigan.

The greatest concentration of ship disappearances on the largest lake, Lake Superior, took place in the early twentieth century during a 12-month period from 1913 to 1914, when six vessels were lost in mysterious or uncertain circumstances. The first two disappeared in the Big Blow of November 1913; they were the British-built ocean freighter *Leafield* and the 525-foot lake freighter *Henry B. Smith*.

The *Leafield*, bound for Thunder Bay, was seen by the passenger liner *Hamonic* only 14 miles from her destination. As Captain Baird of the *Hamonic* watched, the other vessel, fighting her way through the great storm, rose on a huge wave, disappeared into a trough— and evidently never rose again. For the first two days of that storm the *Henry B. Smith* lay in Marquette harbor; then, on November 9, Captain James Owen decided to sail with his cargo of iron ore. Other mariners in the harbor, including Captain Cleary of the Life Saving Service, shook their heads. Owen, however, con-

The *Waubuno*, shown here at her Collingwood dock, figured in one of the classic mysteries of the Lakes. (Courtesy Landon Collection, University of Western Ontario)

Over the years, many vessels have "sailed away" and never been seen again. One of them was the *Alpena*, which sailed into what has come to be known as the "*Alpena* Storm" of October 15-16, 1880, on Lake Michigan. She and the 80 or more people aboard her disappeared. (Courtesy Marine Historical Collection, Milwaukee Public Library)

The *Manistee*, pictured here in winter ice, traded along the southern shore of Lake Superior. After waiting during a November storm for six days in the harbor of Bayfield, Wisconsin, in 1883, the captain became impatient and took her out on the 16th. She was never seen again, although wreckage washed ashore for the next six months. (Courtesy Marine Historical Collection, Milwaukee Public Library)

vinced that the storm had passed, steamed out of harbor as twilight approached. Soon afterward the *Smith* was seen to alter her course abruptly by 90 degrees, either to face a violent wind head-on or perhaps to turn back to harbor. Snow and darkness closed in and no one ever saw her again. Patrols on the beach soon found wreckage, a life raft, and even a seven-foot-square piece of deckhouse. After the storm fishermen discovered flotsam along a 20-mile stretch of coastline. Over the next several months the bodies of the second cook and the first

mate were recovered. That was all.

In the early morning of the following April 28, the captain of a large freighter watched the lights of two smaller vessels off Knife Island, a few miles out of Duluth, as all three ships passed through a gale whose waves put out of commission even the foghorn and light on the Duluth south pier. There were heavy rain squalls, so when the lights of one ship disappeared he assumed that a squall had blanketed them and thought no more of it. But the ship that he saw was apparently the *Benjamin Noble*, a 239-foot carrier designed especially for cargoes of railroad iron, for the *Noble* with such a cargo disappeared that night. For the next few days her wreckage washed ashore near Duluth.

In November 1914 the old lumber steamer *C. F. Curtis*, towing two barges, the *Annie M. Peterson* and *S. K. Marvin*, encountered a northwest snow storm off

Grand Marais. The lifesavers at that port could hear the whistle of the steamer as she sought the entrance to the harbor with her tow, but the wild blizzard was blowing so strongly that evidently the answering sound of the foghorn was carried away and could not be heard aboard the vessel. Next morning lifesavers patrolling the beach found quantities of wreckage with bodies strewn amongst it. A total of 19 bodies, all from the *Curtis* and *Peterson*, were discovered over the next three weeks. A week after the wreck a large piece of the *Marvin* was found floating some distance away in Whitefish Bay, but no bodies from her were ever recovered.

Such losses continued over the years. On Lake Michigan in the "Armistice Day Storm" of November 11, 1940, the struggle was grim for Captain Donald Kennedy and the Canadian freighter *Anna C. Minch*, but no one alive knows the details of terror and despair. The ship was last seen passing through the Straits of Mackinac, bound for Chicago. The bodies of her crew came ashore near Pentwater and Ludington, Michigan, half way down the lake on the east shore, and the forward half of the steamer was later found on the bottom off Pentwater. The after end was completely missing. Kennedy and 12 others of his crew of 24 were from the small Georgian Bay towns of Collingwood and Midland, Ontario. Their loss made a sad impact on those two neighboring communities—a fact no doubt heavy on the mind of the ship's owner, Captain Scott Misener, as he plodded the Lake Michigan beaches looking for identifiable wreckage and bodies.

The *Novadoc*, her back broken and sheathed in ice, after going aground on Lake Michigan near Ludington in the storm of November 11, 1940. The *Novadoc's* men, luckier than some others, were taken off by a fishing boat. (Courtesy Dossin Great Lakes Museum)

The *Anna C. Minch*, in calm waters here, went down on Lake Michigan with all hands in the "Armistice Day Storm" of November 11, 1940. (Courtesy Hamilton Collection, Rutherford B. Hayes Library)

2

Victorian and Edwardian Wrecks of the Canadian Shore

The snow-covered wreck of the *Algoma*.
(Courtesy Public Archives of Canada)

From the last years of Queen Victoria's reign until the First World War, the place of shipping was unique in the world. Those years shaped the ideas many people still have of marine travel, partly because ships were so important then and partly because such authors as Conrad, Kipling and Masefield were writing about them. We still are apt to think of seafaring in their terms.

There were no airliners in the skies or automobile roads along the shores. Trains competed with ships in only a few locations. Ships were usually the best and often the only way to travel or to carry cargo long distances, and they were becoming increasingly efficient. Sailing vessels still existed, but the age of technology had begun. Thus far, the steamship was one of its most successful products.

It was a time when the mariner had good ships, but little more navigational help than he had had for centuries. Primitive radio came into use only toward the end of the period and then sparsely, and such aids as radar and echo sounding were far in the future. Because of the peculiar circumstances, many of the worst wrecks of the best ships took place during these years, on the Great Lakes as elsewhere.

On Saturday, November 7, 1885, in Eagle Pass in the Candian Rockies, the Honorable Donald Smith, dressed in the full costume of a Victorian gentleman, drove the last spike in the construction of the Canadian Pacific Railway, linking eastern and western Canada. Smith, who was more adept at handling millions of dollars than sledge hammers, bent the first spike; it was quickly replaced with a fresh one which he drove home neatly. Earlier that day, unknown to Smith, the Canadian Pacific steamer *Algoma* had crashed into the shore of Greenstone Island off Isle Royale in Lake Superior. Thus, the Canadian Pacific experienced triumph and disaster on the same day.

The first Canadian Pacific steamship service was inaugurated on the Great Lakes in 1884, before the company branched out into either the Atlantic or the Pacific trades. Three fine, steel, propeller-driven steamers were built on the Clydeside in Scotland and sailed across the Atlantic to the St. Lawrence, where they were cut in half and taken through the small canals of those days, being put together again at Buffalo, above the Welland Canal. The vessels combined the most advanced shipbuilding practices of the world-famous Scottish yards with the design characteristics set by Henry Beatty, a member of a Great Lakes shipping family who became manager of the C.P.R. Steamship Line. They were the finest lake steamers that the 1880s could produce.

Toward the end of the second season they were on the Lakes, one of them, the *Algoma*, left Owen Sound, Ontario, on her regular run up Lakes Huron and Superior. On the night of Friday, November 6, Captain John Moore took the 365-foot ship up Lake Superior under both steam and sails—like most steamers of the day, she had masts and sails to help the engines in a fair wind and to steady her in a seaway. She continued through freezing rain, sleet and snow as the wind behind her increased in strength. By 4:00 on Saturday morning, as they were nearing the head of the lake, it had reached gale force. The captain checked down the engines and had sail taken in. When the task was nearly complete he ordered the wheel hard over to starboard, intending to head back into the open lake and wait until visibility improved, as it probably would after daylight.

As the black hull swung around in the dark water, there was a sudden crash of steel against rock. She struck at the stern and immediatley became unmanageable—apparently the rudder was damaged—and, as the captain later reported, she was "driven in by the heavy sea," settling on the bottom just off Greenstone Island at 4:40 A.M., "the seas making a clean breach over her all the time and smashing the ship up."

A 20-year-old dining room waiter ran up on the hurricane deck and saw the captain blowing off the steam to prevent a possible boiler explosion.

The captain told us there was great danger and the safest place was down on the lower decks. We started to run

Advertising poster featuring the "perfect safety" of the *Algoma*. (Courtesy Marine Museum of the Upper Lakes)

there, when the waves carried away the hurricane deck and we grasped the rigging. The captain passed a life line along and we hung on to it for over eight hours, believing that every minute would be our last. It was dark and freezing cold with a terrible sea. There were two ladies and three little girls that I noticed. They were swept away with the cabins, before which we could hear the ladies and girls calling piteously for help but no one could help them. After a while their voices ceased and we all knew they were out in the cruel lake. The cabin was broken completely away in ten minutes after the boat struck.

According to one passenger who had spent three years as a sailor on the Atlantic:

The waves rushed in great mountains over the decks and every few minutes the despairing shriek of some unfortunate persons was heard as they were carried out to sea and lost. The vessel laid broadside to the island and there was a dreadful surf—an awful sea pounding and beating against her sides. The cabin soon gave way and the women, children and men were then washed off the boat beyond all hopes of safety. A great many persons grew almost crazy and jumped into the sea in the hopes of getting ashore. We did not know where we were at first as it was quite dark and there was a terrible storm of sleet and snow blowing in on us. The electric lights went out a few minutes after the boat struck and the confusion and excitement was terrible. The captain alone remained cool and steady. . . . When it seemed certain death to run a life line along the deck he seized a rope and strung out the line, telling the excited people to hold on to the rope and not become panic stricken. High rocks towered up in front of us and the pitiless sea tried to snatch us in its icy clasp on every other side. In this manner we passed the night until it was fairly daylight, the waves dashing over us every few seconds and tearing some one away from the life rope. I was standing between the captain and another man when the cabin came crashing down on the captain and pinned him to the ground. . . . The man on the other side received a severe blow on his head and cried out, "I'm crushed, I'm gone!" The next great wave carried him off without the slightest struggle and he went to his death without a groan.

At about 6:00 A.M. the hull broke in two just forward of the boilers and the forward end of it carried away and sank in deep water, taking with it many of those aboard. The survivors clung to the after end all day Saturday. "Although it was madness to leap through the angry surf to dry land, several determined fellows made the effort, with life preservers. Only

After the *Algoma* struck during a November storm in 1885, this was all that remained of her. (Courtesy Michigan Technological University Library, Houghton)

three landed. The others were hurled against the rocks with tremendous force and mangled beyond recognition."

Gradually the stern section was carried in by the waves until it rested firmly on the bottom. The survivors huddled close together on what had been the steerage deck, wrapped in some blankets they found there. As the passenger described it:

> No one felt inclined to talk, but we sat and looked with anxious eyes at each other, listening to the awful swish! swash! of the merciless waves as they tore along the decks and broke the bulwarks in pieces. Before we rolled the captain up he said, "Men, let us unite in prayer," and with death staring us in the face we knelt down and the captain prayed for us all. Night came on and there seemed no hope. The sea kept bursting over the vessel. The night was spent in darkness with nothing to eat or drink. During the night we could hear the captain enquire from the spot where he lay, a prisoner to his injuries, "How's the wind, mate?" and he seemed glad when he was told that it was veering around to the shore side.

By Sunday morning the weather had moderated. The men on the wreck were able to throw a line to those who had reached the island during the storm. Then, using a makeshift raft, towed back and forth by the line, those aboard were ferried to shore. The captain, who was unable to stand, and another man who held him were the first to go ashore. Altogether there were 14 survivors. Commercial fishermen saw the group and took them to shelter in a nearby cabin. There they stayed Sunday night.

At 5:00 Monday morning the fishermen "brought over their fish tug and asked the captain what was best to be done." He told them to intercept the *Athabasca*, another C.P.R. liner that would be passing. "They did so and the officers came over to the island on the tug for us about an hour after daylight."

The *Athabasca* took the survivors aboard and proceeded to Port Arthur, arriving in the early evening. According to one news reporter, "Up stairs lay Captain Moore, of the ill-fated vessel, terribly crushed and bruised, and in the saloon were the first and second mates, showing plain traces of the awful struggle they had for life with the merciless waters of Lake Superior. Down in the hold were the bodies of two of the men who met an untimely end in their attempt to fight through the surf to land."

Forty-five lives had been lost. The loss on the vessel would be set at $225,000 and on the cargo at $17,000. An official investigation later found that the cause of the wreck was "the ship overrunning her estimated distance, and the failure of the officers to use the log as they should have done." The certificate of Captain Moore, who had eventually recovered, was suspended for nine months and that of the first mate for six months.

Before the Coast Guards of Canada and the United States owned icebreaking vessels with which to clear channels, and before radar and radio direction finders were common, ships usually stopped moving before the end of December. Voyages even in December could be hazardous. If there was a wreck, the lot of survivors would be difficult in sub-zero weather, especially if rescue did not follow quickly. In the wilder parts of the Lakes region, before modern communications and aircraft, castaways might wait indefinitely before they were found.

The 240-foot Canadian wooden steamer *Monarch* left port for the last time at 5:25 on the cold afternoon of Thursday, December 6, 1906. She steamed out of Port Arthur harbor into Lake Superior, carrying her usual crew of 32, plus 12 passengers. In her holds were grain, flour, and general cargo, including two carloads of canned salmon. A fair breeze from the northwest helped her along. Her destination was Sarnia, Ontario, her home port at the foot of Lake Huron, where she had been built by John Dyble in 1890.

She arrived off Thunder Cape at 6:28 P.M. and Captain Edward Robertson altered course, heading toward Passage Island. On passing Thunder Cape the crew streamed the log.

Snow was falling and heavy steam was rising from the water. Visibility was poor, but as they approached the island the men in the wheelhouse twice caught glimpses of Passage Island light ahead. The usual time for the vessel to travel from Thunder Cape to the island was two hours and twenty minutes. Near the end of that time the second mate went aft to check the log and found that it had frozen after registering only 10 miles. Snow and fog had closed in and a heavy sea was running. The northwest wind would carry the sound of the Passage Island fog horn away from the ship, so that those aboard could not hear it. When the two hours and twenty minutes had expired, the captain changed course to the usual one for Whitefish Point, near the far end of the lake. Six minutes later he adjusted the course "to allow for leeway"— an indication perhaps that he was not sure of his position.

A melodramatic account in one newspaper of the day states that Captain Robertson discovered that his compass had been rendered useless by the sub-zero cold and "almost at the same time it dawned upon him that he had lost his bearings." Accordingly, trusting "to his eyesight and providence," the captain stood on the bridge "with his face to the full brunt of the storm and endeavored to regain his course." This account should be taken with some reservation. If they knew before the wreck that the compass was out of order, it would certainly have been to the advantage of all concerned to put that fact in the official report—the "Marine Protest"—signed by the captain and other officers. It does not appear there.

Instead, apparently without warning, about 9:30 P.M. the vessel struck on Isle Royale, two miles west of Blake's Point—well off her supposed course.

"I was standing on the bridge," the captain later said, "when I heard a ripping sound and a part of the upper cabins were torn away."

Many of the passengers had gone to their staterooms. One of them, R. M. Lochead, later related:

> I was sound asleep when the steamer struck. The shock awoke me, but I thought nothing of it. I heard noises and the rush of many feet. I could also hear the passing of orders, but thought the boat had landed at some isolated port and was probably discharging or taking on cargo.
>
> Suddenly the electric lights went out and then I knew that something had gone wrong. I got out of bed, jumped into my clothes, and out upon the deck. My first step on the deck took me into cold water. The roar of the dashing waves on the rocky shore was deafening. Not a man was in sight, but I could hear the tramping of feet on the deck above me.
>
> Then I knew we were wrecked. I seemed to be the only one on the cabin deck, and, realizing the possible danger I

was in, hurriedly made my way to the hurricane deck, where the excitement recalled even at this time all the stories I had read of shipwreck and disaster at sea.

The cold was intense. About forty feet distant the rugged shore line, ice-clad and uninviting, loomed broadside of the steamer.

The wooden steamer *Monarch*, launched at Sarnia, Ontario, in 1890. (Courtesy Dossin Great Lakes Museum)

When the *Monarch* struck, someone on the bridge—presumably the captain—signalled "full speed astern" to the engine room, but Chief Engineer Samuel Beatty apparently realized the extent of damage to the hull and instead kept the engines moving ahead so as to hold the steamer against the shore.

After the initial confusion, the passengers waited quietly while the crew tried to get a line to shore in the darkness and wind-driven snow. First they launched a lifeboat with four men in it; but the churning, breaking seas and the high, rocky, ice-covered shore prevented it from landing. The men had to scramble back aboard the ship. Evidently a smaller rowboat was launched at about the same time, with even less effect.

Then an athletic man named Jack McCallum, who was not a regular seaman but a temporary member of the crew and a brother of the first mate, volunteered to go over the bow on a line. He tied it around his waist, was lowered on the end of it, and, swinging like a pendulum, was able after a couple of tries to gain a foothold on some sacks of grain and mattresses that those on board had thrown out.

A ladder was lowered to him and with it he climbed the tall, ice-sheathed rock to the snowy forest above, reaching the top about half a minute before the ship slid backward a short distance toward deeper water. The boats were described as being "smashed," but they evidently were in such condition that they could be used in running a heavier line ashore. McCallum made it fast to a tree and those aboard began to go along it to the shore or into one of the boats and then ashore. When about half the people were off the wreck, the stern of the ship began to sink, then broke off.

In the darkness James Jacques, a deck watchman, slid down one of the fender ropes, apparently thinking it led to a boat; the rope ended in midair instead, and he fell into the icy water amidst the wreckage and was lost. Jacques had suffered intermittent attacks of blindness and for two days had been unable to see objects more than three or four feet away, a condition that probably contributed to his confusion and death.

The only woman aboard was Miss Rae McCormick, the stewardess. According to the captain, ". . . she was a good one. She went down that rope thirty feet, hand over hand, into the boat without a word." One can imagine her, clad in the ankle-length skirts of the Edwardian era. A passenger remarked that she was the best man in the party. All got ashore that evening except Captain Robertson, who stayed with the tilted, shattered wreck until morning. The same passenger reported, "one crippled axe had been taken off the wrecked steamer, and with this we chopped logs for fires. In watches we spread ourselves out before the cheering blaze." They huddled together in the bitter cold for the rest of the night.

Friday morning the people from the *Monarch* began to organize themselves for a long wait, if necessary, before rescue. They divided into three camps, each of which had that essential for warmth, a fire. They also built a fire as a beacon on the point opposite Passage Island, in hopes that the lighthouse keeper there or a passing ship would see it. Some of them found a case of salmon that had floated ashore and later in the day a few of the men reboarded the wreck and brought off "a quantity of damaged bacon, bread, and pie." They also brought ashore the sails that steamers in those days still carried and used them for makeshift tents to block the wind.

One of the crew members, John Skinner, was an amateur photographer. He managed to get his camera ashore and to take pictures of the wreck.

Friday ended with hunger abated and with fires burning to warm people from the freezing weather and to provide a beacon—but no one saw their beacon that night. On Saturday

Captain Edward Robertson with the purser and steward of the *Monarch*, about 1900. (Courtesy Sarnia Public Library)

morning they were hungry again. Some additional cases of salmon had come ashore from the wreck and the men also found a bag of flour, partly water soaked, on the shore. The able Miss McCormick undertook to do her best with it. "And the way she stirred up that flour with a stick and made up pancakes was a caution," said the captain afterward. The pancakes gave sustenance even though they were not what the stewardess might have produced under better conditions. One passenger saved a pancake as a souvenir and later showed it to a news reporter who wrote, "It was not extra well done, and in appearance resembled a piece of frozen asphalt block."

Saturday night arrived, cold and dark and discouraging, with no sign of rescue. Again they lit their beacon and again they spent the night huddled miserably around the campfire.

On Sunday four crew members set off through the bush to Tobin's Harbor, a sheltered fishing harbor on the opposite side of the island, where there was a commercial fishing camp. Finding the buildings deserted, they stayed in them overnight. They also discovered some food there.

On Saturday night, however, the people at the Passage Island lighthouse had seen the beacon fire and on Sunday the assistant keeper, "rowing a leaky boat three miles in a winter's gale," went to Blake's Point to investigate. He succeeded in taking off the purser of the *Monarch*, Reginald Beaumont. Beaumont had to wade and swim some 100 yards out to the boat through the icy breakers. It is understandable that the rest of the castaways decided to remain where they were until help came.

The *Monarch* struck on Isle Royale in a December snowstorm; her after half then broke off. (Courtesy Dossin Great Lakes Museum)

Some time later one of the lightkeepers was able to signal the passing steamer *Edmonton*, which also was bound eastward from Port Arthur, and to row out and tell Captain McMaster of that steamer what had happened to the *Monarch*. The *Edmonton* obviously could not get to a place on Isle Royale that even the lightkeeper's boat was unable to reach closely, so she turned around and headed back to Port Arthur with the news, arriving there about 2:00 in the morning.

A Mr. Bell, local agent of the Northern Navigation Company, owners of the *Monarch*, immediately began to organize a rescue party and at 6:00 that morning—Monday—the tugs *James Whalen* and *Laura Grace* left for the wreck, carrying rescuers including two doctors. They went first to the Passage Island lighthouse, picked up Purser Beaumont, who had rested there, and with him as pilot steamed across to Isle Royale. There they found that with waves breaking against the wreck and on the shore, it was not possible to land. The *Whalen* gave the castaways a blast of the whistle and the tugs proceeded to Tobin's Harbor, where they found the four men who had gone there the day before. The rest of the party to be rescued had to plod there through the icy winter bush. "We had to walk eight miles before we could get to the tugs," the captain said. ". . . that woman walked through the woods with the best of them. I was on my face half the time." One passenger, "an old man named Farquhar," was badly frostbitten and exhausted by exposure. The crew members took turns carrying him. Most of the rest of the group were in surprisingly good condition.

When the two tugs got back to Port Arthur about 7:00 Monday evening, a large group of friends and relatives of those aboard the *Monarch* were waiting. Mr. Farquhar was taken to the hospital (he was released the following day) and most of the other people from the wreck went to the steamer *Huronic*, which had arrived in port that afternoon. The captain went to the Algoma Hotel, which became a center of activity. After Captain Robertson slowly "crawled into his chair" in the dining room, the management locked the doors to keep out all but a few of his friends who were with him. "The fingers on his right hand were frozen, and his toes, he said, were also frostbitten." Later in the evening, "the old captain went wearily to his room and after a bath he went to bed but sleep would not come to his eyes. After tossing about trying, a doctor had to be brought, who gave him a quieting potion to make him sleep."

The wreck naturally brought H. H. Gildersleeve, manager of the Northern Navigation Company, hurrying to Port Arthur. He did not endear himself to the *Monarch*'s passengers by announcing, "No compensation will be offered by the Northern Navigation Company to passengers who lost their

Another view of the wrecked *Monarch*. (Courtesy Ontario Archives)

effects on the wrecked steamer *Monarch*. That is one of the risks taken by passengers and they have no case for damages against the company." He provided transportation eastward for the passengers on the *Huronic* and paid the hospital and doctor's bills of Mr. Farquhar, but commented that even these things were more than the company was legally required to do. After talking with the captain about the condition of the wreck, Mr. Gildersleeve abandoned the ship to the underwriters, notifying them by telegram.

The townspeople of Port Arthur and neighboring Fort William were sympathetic to Captain Robertson. On Wednesday evening a group of dignitaries gathered in the dining room of the Algoma Hotel to honor him. Among them were the mayor, city councilmen and presidents of the Port Arthur and Fort William boards of trade. President George Mooring of the Port Arthur board opened the proceedings "with an address eulogistic of Captain Robertson, and expressive of the sympathy of his Port Arthur friends." President John Lumby of the Fort William board then read a prepared statement reviewing Captain Robertson's 35-year career on the Lakes as ample proof of his ability, and asking him to accept "the accompanying purse of gold as a token of our friendship, and we all desire to see you back to these ports sailing even a bigger and better ship." Captain Robertson replied that "he doubly appreciated their kindness and good will in the day of his misfortune." The whole tenor of the meeting implied that those present feared that Captain Robertson's long maritime career was ended. And in fact he never sailed again.

The meeting also expressed high appreciation for the heroic service of John McCallum in getting the line ashore and providing a way of escape from the wreck, and recommended that he receive official recognition. About six months later— on the evening of July 2, 1906—the Port Arthur Board of Trade met in the chamber of the city council and presented McCallum with the bronze medal of the Royal Canadian Humane Society, for heroism displayed at the time of the wreck. He later received a payment of $50 in lieu of another medal from the Department of Marine and Fisheries in Ottawa.

*W*hat caused the wreck? Apparently no official investigation was held. For that reason we can only surmise the causes from the information that we have. There was criticism in the Canadian press at the time because the U.S. Government had not marked *both* sides of the channel and placed a light on Blake's Point as well as the one on Passage Island. To that the Canadian Minister of Marine and Fisheries replied: ". . . as the gap between Passage Island and Isle Royale is three miles wide

The wrecked *Monarch* from a different angle. The wreck pictures were taken by John Skinner, a member of the crew. (Courtesy Rev. Edward J. Dowling, S.J.)

and as Passage Island shore is perfectly safe there ought to be no necessity for marking both sides of the passage. If you will call to mind other similar passages you will find that it is the invariable practice to mark only the safest side."

Shortly after the wreck occurred, a doctor who had been a passenger on the *Monarch* the preceding October wrote to the Minister of Marine and Fisheries, recounting a conversation he had overheard on that voyage between the captain and the man at the wheel. As the doctor described it, it went: "Captn—Bert, we should be near such and such a light. Bert says well 'there it is.' The Captn answers where? Bert answers 'Just abreast of us.'" The doctor went on to say, "I would not like to think that Captn Robertson was responsible for the accident. Yet I am constrained to write the department of the preceding incident. It would appear to me that Captn Robertson is aged. I would like to ask if there is any age limit? Or if there is exacted from each master of a passenger ship accurate vision?"

The ministry answered that once a master was licensed, there was no re-examination and that "it rests entirely with the owners of the vessel who they should employ as master." But the ministry also sent out instructions to have the captain's eyesight tested, although no record has been found to show that this was actually done. The captain was ill at his home in Sarnia, having had the big toe of his right foot amputated as an aftermath of frostbite. It probably was plain that he never would command another ship, and for that reason the matter may have been dropped.

It is tempting to blame the wreck on the captain's poor eyesight, but on the night of the accident, just as at the time of the doctor's voyage, there certainly were other eyes in the wheelhouse. Poor visibility caused by snow and by fog rising from the water certainly contributed to the disaster. The captain, who had commanded the ship since she was commissioned 16 years earlier, said that his only explanation for the disaster was that the compass must have been at fault, and it well may have been. All we can definitely say is that the *Monarch* strayed from her course in a December storm.

The 195-foot steam yacht *Gunilda* struck a shoal in Nipigon Bay, Lake Superior, after her owner refused to hire a local pilot.

The steel yacht *Gunilda,* 195 feet long, was built in Leith, Scotland, for William Lamont Harkness, son of a partner of John D. Rockefeller. She was a typical steam yacht of that era, long and slim, painted white, with clipper bow and counter stern. Harkness brought *Gunilda* to the Great Lakes in 1910 and cruised the north shore of Lake Superior then and in the following year. In the summer of 1911 he decided to explore Nipigon Bay, a poorly charted extension of the lake. The master of the yacht, Captain Corkum, felt that they should

Side view of the grounded *Gunilda*. As she was being pulled off, she rolled over and sank in 300 feet of water. (Both, courtesy Rev. Edward J. Dowling, S.J.)

take aboard a local pilot before exploring the bay. A local man offered to do the job for $15. The wealthy Harkness angrily rejected the offer as too expensive. The next day another man said that he would pilot her in for $25 and was even more brusquely refused.

Steaming toward the bay, *Gunilda* without warning ran up on McGarvey Shoal, marked on Canadian charts but not on the American chart that the yacht carried. She was moving so briskly that she slid up on the shoal until nearly 50 feet of her was completely out of water. She was sturdily built and was not damaged, but there was no way her crew could get her off unaided. Her owner, his wife and children, his three guests and most of the crew of 21 went glumly ashore and caught a train at the nearby town of Rossport.

In due course Captain James Whalen of the Port Arthur towing firm was hired by the New York underwriters who had insured the *Gunilda* and was instructed to get her off the reef. He had no sooner arrived at the scene with the tug *James Whalen*—the same one that had rescued the *Monarch* passengers four years previously—than Harkness himself came in by train and had one of the local fishermen take him out to the salvage tug. Whalen, fearing that the yacht would heel when he pulled her off, decided that he should return to Port Arthur and get two scows to lash on either side of her so she could not roll over. Even though the insurance company was paying the salvagers, Harkness saw this as merely an excuse to charge more. He insisted that Whalen simply pull her straight off the way she had run on. In the face of this demand, Whalen ran cables from the tug to the yacht and pulled. At first nothing happened. Then, on a second try, *Gunilda* slowly moved off the shoal, tilted to starboard, and gently sank out of sight in 300 feet of water.

3

Wrecks of the American Shore
1885-1910

The *David Wallace* (left) and *Robert Wallace* drove onto the Chocolay Reefs near Marquette, Michigan. (Courtesy Rev. Edward J. Dowling, S.J.)

During the latter 1800s and early 1900s, a great deal of bulk cargo moved along the American side of the Lakes. Lake freighters, in much the same form that would persist for nearly a century—long, flat-sided vessels with wheelhouses forward and engines aft—had evolved to carry such cargoes. Often they towed other vessels. At first the towed vessels were schooners that were thus hurried on their way; later they were unpowered barges built especially for the purpose, so that shipowners would save the cost of an extra engine for the second vessel. Such carriers moved ore down the Lakes from Superior and northern Lake Michigan to furnaces and mills on the more populous shores. They carried coal back to northwestern ports. Lumber steamers took eastward the products of dwindling forests. There was a growing flow eastward, on both the U.S. and Canadian sides, of grain coming from the developing prairie states and provinces. Commerce and the bulk freight it brought were concentrated on the American side. Most of the vessels moving along the American shores were freighters and as a result most of the disasters there involved freighters.

The steamer *Robert Wallace*, towing the schooner *David Wallace*, set out from Duluth in clear weather on November 15, 1886, bound down the Lakes for Buffalo. Both the 209-foot steamer and the 217-foot schooner were laden with wheat. On the 16th, a northeasterly gale began—one that would cause some 30 wrecks before it ceased. By the 17th the two *Wallaces* were in the middle of Lake Superior, in blinding snow, punching into winds of 45 miles per hour. Eventually the ships turned and ran before the gale. Near midnight Captain Frank H. Brown of the steamer realized that he must be nearing shore and checked down his engine, hoping to find his way into shelter. He was moving slowly ahead, the two vessels nearly out of control in the storm, when at 1:00 A.M. his ship went hard aground. The schooner veered to one side, passed the steamer, then swung around and grounded nearer shore.

The vessels had struck the Chocolay Reefs a few miles southeast of Marquette, Michigan. A lifesaving station had not yet been established there. Several local volunteers took a yawl boat by wagon to the beach opposite the wreck, manned the boat and tried to row out to the stricken vessels. They made several efforts; each time the pounding seas drove them back.

Next, someone thought of an old mortar that was kept at a Marquette powder mill. It could be used to fire a line to the vessels. As it turned out, the mortar—perhaps a Civil War trophy—had been spiked, and the touch-hole had to be redrilled. By the time this was done and the mortar was finally brought to the beach, it was dusk. The men duly loaded and prepared the weapon by the light of bonfires. It fired with a dull explosion, throwing the line 50 feet out into the water. Quickly some of them drew the line back and re-coiled it while others reloaded the gun with a considerably larger charge. Again they fired it. This time the explosion was sufficiently authentic, but the mortar burst and sent fragments whistling in all directions. Luckily, no one was hurt.

During the storm Captain John Frink of the little harbor tug *Gillett* had been a busy man. The preceding day, as the storm had grown worse, he had towed one schooner into harbor and a little later had taken the crew off another schooner that was drifting ashore. But the *David Wallace* and *Robert Wallace* were too far from harbor and the storm was now too strong for his tug to attempt to reach them. During the day, as the amateur efforts to help the vessels went on, Frink telegraphed the nearest lifesaving station, which was at Portage Entry, near Houghton, Michigan, 110 miles to the west. The message was taken by tug from Houghton to the station, which was six miles away on the Portage Ship Canal. Albert Ocha, keeper of the station, received it at 4:00 P.M.

Ocha's crew loaded their lifeboat and other gear on the tug, which took them back to Houghton. There Superintendent Hornby of the Marquette, Houghton and Ontonogon Railroad had a special train waiting with the line's fastest engine, Number 39, and its crack engineer, Henry Jackson. The lifesavers, with the help of volunteers from town, loaded their equipment on the two flatcars and climbed into the one passenger car that made up the three-car train. It plunged into the blizzard at 7:45 P.M.

A scheduled run between Houghton and Marquette took nine and a half hours. Jackson got the train there over the snow-covered track in three hours and ten minutes. It reached Marquette, where it paused briefly, then steamed on to a point nearest Chocolay Beach, where Captain Frink had wagons waiting. There a crowd helped unload the lifeboat and gear and take them to the shore where several bonfires were burning.

First, Captain Ocha tried to fire a line to one of the vessels with his Lyle gun. Accounts vary; some say that he missed in the darkness, others that the line reached one of the ships, but that the crew would not venture out onto their dark, storm-washed deck to retrieve it. The rudder of the lifeboat had been damaged sometime during the trip, but by 2:00 A.M. it was repaired. The lifesavers launched the boat with the help of many volunteers, but either in the launching or soon afterward the iron strapping on the rudder bent and the wood split. By the time the boat reached the first reef it had filled with water three times. Ocha ordered it back to shore. Repairs began again on the rudder while Ocha tried once more to reach one of the ships with his Lyle gun, but to no avail.

At daybreak they launched the boat again, and the oarsmen pulled away toward the steamer. Seas washed into the lifeboat; part of the crew had to bail steadily while the others rowed. After seeming to disappear several times during the long, hard row, the lifeboat reached the steamer and pulled into her lee. Ocha loaded nine of her crew into the boat and brought them back to shore. The return trip was relatively easy. The boat went again into the storm to take the remaining six men off the steamer and bring them ashore. It went back a third time to the schooner. The oarsmen were nearly exhausted. On that trip the boat was almost thrown end over end and the rudder was split once more, but Ocha steered by giving commands to the men at the oars. Several times the boat was flooded by the waves and was bailed out. It arrived at the schooner about 8:00 A.M., took off the crew of nine, and by 9:30 that morning all the shipwrecked sailors were ashore. The ice-encrusted lifesavers were in worse condition than the men they had rescued; they were taken to the bonfires and given hot coffee and food.

The ships were later refloated. They spent the winter in Marquette harbor and the next spring were towed to Detroit for extensive repairs.

At nearly the opposite end of the Great Lakes, on Lake Ontario, Oswego, N.Y., had a busy harbor where many schooners called. The sailing vessels usually had to be towed in and out of port, thus supporting a small fleet of tugs.

The Canadian two-master *Flora Emma,* 98 feet long on deck, carrying a cargo of lumber, was tied up at the western end of the harbor on the night of November 15, 1893. While most of the crew were ashore, a sudden westerly came up. As a crew member on another Canadian schooner there put it, "It came on to blow from the westward, driving a great sea down the lake. You know how it blows up at Oswego." The *Flora Emma* broke loose and drifted eastward through the snow squalls. Captain Thomas Fox and one of his sons got an anchor out, but it dragged on the rocky bottom. The wind and current from the Oswego River carried the vessel out of the harbor toward the shoreline to the east, where breakers foamed dangerously and a pier thrust out to form an added hazard.

The tug *Eliza J. Redford* was docked at the eastern end of the harbor near the lifesaving station. Her master, Captain Henry Featherstonehaugh—"a fair-complexioned chap with a dark moustache and a saucy style"—took her out to get the *Flora Emma.* By then it was 11:00 P.M., "pitch black and the lake roaring like a cage of lions at feeding time."

Captain Fox later recalled:

> When the tug came out she made a circle on the outside of us, but could not get a line to the vessel. I then saw that he could not complete the turn and bring his head to the sea, as he was too near the pier. I heard her back up and thought she was going to back out to us but he went ahead again. The captain could not turn his tug this time either. Then I heard an explosion and realized that the tug had been disabled and that we both were gone.

The tug and the schooner were blown toward land. The schooner drove ashore beside the pier. Meanwhile, Captain Fox was moving quickly.

> I ran to the cabin and pulled my wife out and after a hazardous experience got her forward near the forecastle. The seas were breaking over us and the lumber was coated with ice, and it was no easy task to take a woman the whole length of the vessel. The life crew took us off, and I think Captain Featherstonehaugh must have gone overboard when the tug struck the pier.

Captain Anderson, keeper of the lifesaving station, told of the accident as he saw it:

> When the tug got outside, the schooner had drifted out of the new harbor and was about half way to the shore from

the west end of the East pier. The snow came down so thick just at this moment that we could see nothing. I heard two blasts of the whistle and took it for a signal that the tug had abandoned the vessel to us. In a moment the vessel was on the beach. Then we heard an explosion and the air was filled with steam and snow. As were launching the boat to go to the tug, I saw that she had struck the east pier and that the pilot house was gone.

Just then a big sea picked up the tug and rolled her clear in to the beach alongside the schooner. We quickly got out an apparatus, fired a line to the schooner and sent out the breeches buoy. The first person brought ashore was Mrs. Fox, wife of the Captain. The seas had been breaking over the vessel and the woman was wet. When we got hold of her she was unconscious. We next got the Captain's son and then the Captain. The crew of the tug, except for the captain, had in the meantime gotten off on the pier, when the tug struck, but we supposed Captain Featherstonehaugh had got aboard the vessel. Captain Fox said that he had seen nothing of him, however, and then we realized he was gone.

A series of mishaps caused the wreck, perhaps the most important of them being the failure of the tug's steering machinery at a critical moment. Engineer John Connell, who survived, later said:

Wrecks of the schooner *Flora Emma* and the tug *Eliza J. Redford* at Oswego, New York. The picture was taken on November 16, 1893, the day after the night-time wreck. (Courtesy Hamilton Collection, Rutherford B. Hayes Library)

Captain Featherstonehaugh gave orders and was cool and collected to the very last. I was in the engineroom, and when the steering apparatus gave out George Day, who was with me, went out on deck. When the tug struck the pier Day jumped. The crash burst a steam pipe and the hot steam filled the engine room and scalded my breast and lower part of the body. The Captain came aft and told us that there was no use trying to save the tug and told us to get up forward. He stood with one foot on the door of the wheel-house and one foot on the top of the forward tow post.

He told us to get ready to jump and to take a start so that we would be sure to land on the pier. We agreed to jump together. When the tug sagged in against the pier my brother Jerry and myself jumped. We thought Captain Featherstonehaugh jumped also. I did not see him on the pier.

The captain was lost, apparently washed back by the seas after he jumped; he, too, had been badly scalded as was apparent when his body was later recovered. The engineer and his brother were unable to stand on the wave-swept pier, so they crawled on hands and knees to a schooner that was tied up there, and were eventually taken by boat to the lifesaving station. The two wrecked vessels were total losses. "Their planking littered the beach, mixed with the *Flora Emma's* lumber cargo."

Captain Fox of the *Flora Emma* owned his vessel and carried no insurance—not an unusual circumstance in those days. He had lost both his floating home and his business. The local ship chandler, John S. Parsons, passed the hat among the schooner men and raised $214 for him.

Twelve months later Oswego had two more wrecks. On November 24, 1894, the Canadian schooner *Baltic* approached the harbor in a heavy blow, carrying 12,600 bushels of barley from the Bay of Quinte. Captain John T. Beard, her master and owner, sailed his vessel along the coast some distance and then returned, hoping that during that time the wind would moderate. It did not. Because darkness was approaching, he decided he had to enter harbor.

Outside the harbor entrance the tug *Charlie Ferris* stood by to help. But the wind shifted suddenly to the southwest, and before her sails could be trimmed, the schooner was carried away toward the east bank beyond the harbor. The tug turned and ran back into harbor, blowing five long blasts on her whistle to alert the lifesavers.

The lifesaving crew turned out with their equipment and

followed the schooner along the shore until she ran firmly aground. They shot a line to her, but the wind carried it wide of the mark. On the second try they were able to get a line aboard and bring ashore in the breeches buoy all who were aboard—the captain, his wife, his three sons and (reports vary) one or two seamen. Mrs. Beard, unconscious, was taken to the lifesaving station where Mrs. Anderson, wife of the keeper, took care of her. The *Baltic,* which was not insured, began to break up and the nearby beach was covered with barley.

About 5:00 A.M. on the 27th the Oswego schooner *Daniel G. Fort,* commanded by Captain W. J. Gordon, tried to enter port in a fresh breeze. The same tug came out to meet her, got a heaving line to the schooner, and began to haul the tow rope aboard. But something went wrong (again, the accounts vary); the tow rope was not fastened firmly to the tug,

The *Baltic* missed the harbor entrance at Oswego during a November blow; three days later the *Daniel G. Fort* missed the same entrance and came to rest beside the *Baltic.* (Courtesy Marine Historical Collection, Milwaukee Public Library)

and it slipped away again. The schooner was blown eastward and went aground beside the wrecked *Baltic*. (The *Fort*, owned by an Oswego syndicate, was valued at $5,000 and insured for $3,800.)

Once more Captain Anderson and his lifesavers took their gear down the beach and shot a line aboard the schooner, but no one on the vessel paid any attention to it. The lifesavers returned to their station, launched their surfboat and rowed out to the wreck, where they took off the crew. History does not record what they said when they learned that their line had been ignored because all hands were below packing their belongings.

The steel freighter *Sevona*, laden with iron ore, steamed out of the harbor at Superior, Wisconsin, on Friday evening, September 1, 1905. A vessel 372.5 feet long, she had been rebuilt at Buffalo earlier that year and enlarged from her former 300-foot length.

As she left the Allouez docks at Superior and moved into the open lake there was no wind, but heavy ground swells were running. Aboard (in addition to the male crew) were Mrs. William Phillipie, wife of the chief engineer; Louise Cluckey, second cook and wife of the steward; and two young guests, Kate Spencer and Lillian Jones, friends of the family of James McBrier of Erie, Pennsylvania, who was head of the company that owned the ship.

After dinner and a pleasant evening the two guests went to their cabins at the forward end of the vessel about 9:00.

The steamer *Sevona*, lost on Lake Superior in September 1905. (Courtesy Center for Archival Collections, Bowling Green State University)

Captain Donald Sutherland McDonald, as experienced a shipmaster as could be found on the Lakes, turned to his ship's business. Captain McDonald, originally a Scots-Canadian from along the Ontario shore, had been a seaman on the ocean in his youth and had been one of two survivors of a shipwreck on the Irish coast. In time he had returned to fresh water and continued his maritime career there. He was now part owner of the *Sevona*.

The wind began to rise. By midnight it reached gale strength. At 2:00 in the morning the *Sevona* was some 70 miles out of Superior, boring into heavy seas that broke over her bow and ran the length of the deck. The storm was so powerful that Captain McDonald decided to turn and head for shelter behind the Apostle Islands, which lay southwest of his position.

The *Sevona* ran before the gale. At 3:30 the captain woke the two girls and told them to dress. Half an hour later he had four seamen take them aft to the galley, the sailors hanging on to lifelines and escorting the young women through waist-deep waves that washed over the deck. The freighter carried all of her lifeboats aft. Safety rules, which the government had imposed with other kinds of ships in mind, prevented lake freighters of the day from carrying any boats forward. The captain evidently wanted his young guests in a place where lifeboats were available.

As the freighter rushed toward the Apostle Islands before the wild storm, Captain McDonald and the other men in the wheelhouse strained to see Raspberry Island light, but they were blinded by the curtain of driving rain which completely blotted out the island. About 5:45 A.M. the captain realized that they must be near the Apostles and slowed his engines to half speed, hoping to find his way into a sheltered spot. Fifteen minutes later, still running blind, the *Sevona* struck. As Chief Engineer Phillipie later described it, "There were three distinct shocks and crashes when the boat came to a stand and broke in two." She was on Sand Island Shoal—which despite its name is a ridge of solid granite.

Captain McDonald, cut off from the stern section of his command by the break in the hull, called aft through a megaphone, shouting through the wind, directing the men to lower the boats and put the women into them, but to hang on to the freighter as long as possible. The men aft lowered the starboard boat into the water and held it there in the lee of the wreck. They dragged the port boat, on the exposed side, across the deck and succeeded in launching it on the starboard side of the freighter where the hull of the wrecked ship provided a little shelter. Meanwhile, the seven men in the bow section were making a raft from wooden hatch covers and doors.

Chief Engineer Phillipie, now in charge of the stern end of the wreck, soon put the women back in the warm, dry ship's

All that was left of the *Sevona* after she was wrecked in the Apostle Islands. (Courtesy Dossin Great Lakes Museum)

Another view of the *Sevona* wreck. (Courtesy Dossin Great Lakes Museum)

dining room and kept only enough men on deck at any one time to control the floating boats. But the storm increased and by 11:00 that morning the stern section of the wreck began to list. The time had come to leave it. Phillipie took charge of the larger boat, into which the women were placed; deckhand Charles Scouller, who had some small-boat experience, took charge of the other. (In later years, Scouller himself became a captain.) The boats were crewed by an odd assortment of firemen, oilers, engineers and the steward, for most of the seamen were isolated forward of the break in the hull.

Phillipie tried to move his lifeboat up to the forward section, but the big steel-gray waves rolling over the broken center part of the vessel kept washing the boat away and threatening to swamp it. The forward end of the ship stood fast, however, and appeared able to endure the storm; by this time, the men there had taken shelter inside the cabin structure and Phillipie could not see them. So he cast off, his makeshift crew pulling at the oars.

After a harrowing row through the storm, they reached the Wisconsin shore south of the islands, where they were welcomed at a lumber camp, fed, and given places to sleep. The smaller boat drove ashore on Sand Island itself, and there the men in it found an abandoned cabin for shelter and a nearby homesteader who provided food.

Early next morning—Sunday—Phillipie borrowed a horse and wagon from the lumbermen and drove to the small town of Bayfield, 14 miles away, arriving in the late afternoon. He arranged for a fishing tug to go out and, he hoped, rescue the forward-end crew. But as the tug fought its way through the still-heavy seas and came within view of the wreck, he saw with a sinking heart that the bow end of the *Sevona* had completely disappeared. Sadly he turned back to Bayfield.

On Monday the storm had subsided and Phillipie was

able to get a larger tug. It picked up the four men on Sand Island and began the search for the others. In time the bodies of all those who had been on the forward section, including that of Captain McDonald, were found along the beach. The captain was known to be carrying $1500 with which to conduct the ship's business—meeting the payroll, buying supplies and the like—but only a single dollar bill was found on the beach near him. Evidently someone else had discovered his body before the official searchers. Afterward, several questionable local characters were seen to be spending unusually large sums in Bayfield, but nothing was ever proved.

The *Sevona* was a total loss. Her certificate of enrollment was surrendered by her owners two months later.

Captain R. F. Humble had only routine concerns when he headed the steamer *Mataafa,* towing the barge *James Nasmyth,* out of Duluth harbor at 5:00 P.M. on Monday, November 28, 1905. The steamer was 430 feet long, the barge 365 feet long; both were heavily laden with iron ore. Though any shipmaster knows in the back of his mind that disaster can strike without warning, there was nothing to tell the captain that this would be a particularly grim voyage.

When the two ships left harbor there was a fresh wind from the east-northeast, with the temperature near zero, but with little sea. As the *Mataafa* and her consort headed eastward, a blizzard swept over Lake Superior. Blinding snow was carried by winds consistently stronger than 60 miles an hour. As the storm grew, the two ships were battered by the waves and their decks were constantly awash. Because of the snow the men aboard could see no more than a few yards in any direction. About 4:00 A.M., when they were perhaps 20 miles east of Two Harbors, Captain Humble decided that enough was enough. He turned the *Mataafa,* still towing the *Nasmyth,* back toward port and gave strict orders that no one was to venture out on the deck, which was being constantly washed by seas that would carry a man over the side.

It was Tuesday afternoon by the time the laboring ships were again off Duluth. The entrance to Duluth harbor is a short length of narrow canal. Captain Humble saw that in that storm there was no chance of getting both the steamer and her tow back through the narrow harbor entrance, and so he dropped the barge to fend for herself. The morality of cutting loose an unpowered barge in dangerous circumstances was always debatable, and it was a hard decision for the shipmaster to make. Captain Humble later admitted that although the *Nasmyth* had dropped her anchors, he fully expected that she would drag ashore, but felt it was better to try to save one ship than lose two.

About 2:30 that afternoon the *Mataafa* ran for the harbor entrance. Captain Humble aimed her bow at the middle of the opening, but just before she reached it the stern of the steamer was lifted by an exceptionally large wave and her bow, dropping into the trough ahead, struck bottom with a heavy blow. She stumbled in her progress, and the wind and waves carried her just enough off course that she struck the pier and began to swing sideways. The captain signalled the engineer, trying to free her, but when she struck the engines suddenly started to whir and the engineroom crew knew that she had lost her propeller.

The ship was out of control. She swung completely around, finally sweeping up broadside toward the beach and about 600 feet off shore, with huge waves breaking over her.

When the *Mataafa* first hit the pier, a wave carried away one of her lifeboats, and in the ensuing minutes her other boat and her life raft were smashed away. The men aboard her had no way of escaping.

About noon another steamer, the *R. W. England,* had gone aground in the storm about three miles away and the Duluth lifesavers, after a struggle to get along the beach through the wind and sleet of the storm (and over the debris and fallen electrical lines it had caused), were hard at work rescuing her crew. They were not able to respond immediately to the *Mataafa*'s situation. The men aboard the wrecked freighter knew nothing of this, of course, and could not understand why the lifesavers did not appear.

Soon after the steamer took the beach, a sea smashed in her starboard gangway door abreast the engine room and water flooded the after area, forcing the men there out on the weather deck, where they tried to find shelter in the lee of the smoke stack and ventilators. (A peculiarity of the vessel's construction was that she had no real deck cabin aft.) The

Left: While running for shelter the *Mataafa* struck the pierhead at Duluth (note lighthouse at far right)—
Right: And swung sideways across the pier. (Both, courtesy Great Lakes Historical Society)

second mate and three others who were in the after part of the ship decided to go forward. The mate and two of the others fought their way along the deck, watching for the seas and dropping and holding on when they hit, and in this way finally reached the forward structure. The fourth man, a fireman, started forward, but a wave caught him and threw him overboard. He grabbed the lines along the side of the vessel and drew himself on the deck again when the wave had passed—only to be knocked over again. He was knocked overboard three times and each time managed to regain the deck; but then, apparently injured, he crawled back to the lee side of the smokestack.

After the three men reached the forward end, there were 15 crewmen forward and 9 aft. The pilot house was filled with water "up to the neck" and the 15 all crowded into the captain's room.

About an hour and a half after the wreck occurred, constant battering by the waves broke the steel ship in two with a gunshot crack that was clearly heard by the crowds on shore. The stern of the wreck, already the lowest part, began to sink lower. Every so often those crowds saw the captain appear on the forward deck and call out through a megaphone, but the sound of the storm was so great that no words could be heard ashore. Just before dark, during a lull in the storm, they could hear him call, "My God! Can't . . ." and the rest was lost in the rush of wind and waves.

Shortly after 5:00 P.M., when dusk was gathering, the lifesavers arrived and a cheer went up from the crowd—which then promptly gathered around and hindered them in their work. The lifesavers emplaced their Lyle gun and fired two lines to the ship. Each one apparently fell out on the open deck and either no one aboard saw it or no one could reach it because of the breaking waves. They moved the gun and with another shot put a line directly over the pilot house, but then the shot and trail lines became frozen together and tangled. The captain finally cut the shot line, and the lifesavers ashore, who could not see clearly what was happening, thought it had somehow been cut accidentally. They fired other lines aboard, but the men there, numb with cold and working in icy water, were unable to rig the breeches buoy.

The lifesavers worked until nearly midnight, but felt they could not send a boat out because of the combination of rocky beach, huge waves and powerful undertow. Captain Humble later agreed that they were right. He did not comment on other factors: that the lifesaving crew had been up all the previous night saving their own station property from the storm and had already carried out one rescue that subzero day; that they were exhausted, hungry, and in frozen clothing; and that human stamina has its limits.

Aboard the wreck the men in the forward end settled

Top: She hung on the end of the pier. (Courtesy Kenneth Thro)—
Bottom: Then turned completely around and lodged sideways on shore. (Courtesy Marine Historical Collection, Milwaukee Public Library)

Waves battered her while nine men died from drowning or exposure in the after section. (Courtesy Kenneth Thro)

down to a bleak night. There was no heat in the captain's cabin. He had the men collect and light all of the available lamps, so as to generate a little warmth. All of the doors and windows had been knocked out, and water from the waves kept rushing in and freezing as it hit. There was no food and most of the men had not eaten for hours. They were wet to the skin, and kept from freezing only by stamping around. One of them said afterward, "We danced about all night to the tune of that horribly gurgling water." Another added, "It was like an Indian pow-wow." According to Captain Humble:

> It took every effort of myself, the first mate, the second mate, and the wheelsman to keep the balance of the crew standing on their feet and moving about. It was getting colder all the time. About 5 o'clock in the morning the lamps burned out, and I was sure we would freeze before daylight. As a last hope I waded down in the water along the passage way through three or four feet of water to the windlass room, where I secured some kerosene, rags, and dry matches, and by chopping down a bathroom I got some wood with which to build a fire. When I had started the fire I called all hands down. We stood about the fire until 7:30 o'clock, when the lifesaving crew came out in the surfboat.

It was even grimmer in the after end of the ship, for there no one lived through the night, if indeed anyone was left alive when darkness fell.

Next morning at daybreak the lifesavers were on hand with their surfboat. A thick gray mist hung over the water. The black waves still were rolling in at some height and everything the water touched was covered with ice. Just after the surfboat was launched she was hit by a heavy sea that unseated the bow oarsman and filled the boat, but her self-bailing equipment slowly emptied her and the crew pulled on out to the wreck.

Coming alongside, they took aboard seven of the survivors, then turned and pulled back to shore. Just when they were about to land, a big comber struck the boat and drove it against a pile of rocks. Fortunately, the lifesavers were trailing a drogue which acted as a brake on their boat and there was no serious damage to it. The rescued crew members were bundled into waiting carriages and taken to a hotel. About an hour later the remainder of those in the forward end of the ship were taken into the surfboat and brought ashore.

According to a news reporter on the scene, "A glance at the stern of the sunken boat told only too plainly the sad story of those unfortunates who were imprisoned in that part of the vessel by the raging waves. This morning, the stern half of the boat had sunk considerably further than yesterday and even the mildest wave dashed over her at will."

The lifesavers then turned their attention to the after section. There they found only four bodies; the others had either been washed overboard or were in the lower compartments, under water. The frozen body of the fireman who had made the futile attempt to get forward was found lying, with arms outstretched, on the lee side of the smokestack. There also lay the bodies of the chief engineer and the steward, both of whom had fractured skulls—apparently from being thrown against the ship by waves. "The most horrible spectacle was presented by the body of McLeod, the deckhand. He had taken refuge in the ventilator on the lee side of the vessel, and with a hand clutching each side, was peering out toward shore, his sightless eyes and contorted countenance presenting a ghastly sight."

And what of the *Nasmyth*, the barge that was cut loose by the *Mataafa* before running for harbor? Through all of the storm she remained anchored about a mile out, and when it was over she was towed into port, safe and unharmed.

Left: Next morning lifesavers went out to her. Note the surfboat just to the right of the bow section. (Courtesy Rev. Edward J. Dowling, S.J.) Right: Lifesavers bringing ashore members of the *Mataafa's* crew. (Courtesy Ralph K. Roberts).

however, before the *Lafayette* could be salvaged, and only the stern section carrying her engines was saved and taken into Duluth.

The steel freighter *Cyprus* was launched on August 17, commissioned on September 21, and lost (during her second voyage) on October 11, 1907. She was 440 feet long over all, one of a number of sister ships of the same design—and the only one that ever got into serious trouble.

About 9:00 A.M. on Thursday, October 10, Captain F. B. Huyck took the *Cyprus* out of harbor at Superior, Wisconsin. She was bound for Buffalo with slightly more than 7,000 tons of iron ore. By Friday noon there was a considerable sea running from the north-northwest on Lake Superior, but the steamer seemed to be riding well. By late afternoon the wind had risen to gale strength and the seas were heavy, washing continually over the deck. The *Cyprus* was in the trough and was rolling. She also had developed a list to port; there was water in her cargo hold and it had caused the cargo to shift. Captain Huyck kept the pumps operating and held the steamer on her course down Lake Superior toward the shelter of Whitefish Point, which he evidently felt he could reach safely.

The wind and sea continued to increase, and so did the list to port. The crew were near panic, many of them putting on life preservers. Finally, the captain turned the vessel south, toward the nearest land. Shortly before 7:00 P.M. he had the lifeboats cleared and sent all the men aft to stand by them except those members of the forward crew who were on duty. About 7:30 the list became so pronounced that the port rail reached the water. Five minutes later the chief engineer notified the captain that he could no longer keep the engines running. The captain sent all but four men aft to the boats. He, along with the first and second mates and a watchman, decided to stand by the forward life raft. All four of them wore life preservers.

About 7:45 the *Cyprus* rolled over and sank. The four men kept their grip on the raft and were thrown into the water with it; when they came to the surface there was no sign of the ship. They climbed onto the raft and heard some other men calling. Supposing that the others were in one of the boats, they called back, but after a few exchanges of shouts, heard nothing more.

The steamer went down about 18 miles from land. The four men remained on the life raft until around 2:00 the following morning when it drifted into the breakers along the southern shore of the lake. There the waves turned it over, throwing the men into the water. They climbed back on it again—and it tipped over again. The raft turned over four times, the last time when it was about 300 feet off the beach.

The brand-new steamer *Cyprus*. (Courtesy Marine Historical Collection, Milwaukee Public Library)

The last time three of the men disappeared; the fourth, Second Mate Charles G. Pitz, caught hold of the raft but made no effort to get back on it. He let it tow him to shallow water, and when his feet touched bottom he walked and crawled up onto the beach. A lifesaver from the Deer Park station found him there and took him to the station, where the lifesaving crew gave him "stimulants and clothing," and he survived. Of the 23 men aboard the *Cyprus,* he was the only one saved.

Pitz later wrote a letter thanking Keeper McGaw and his men of the Deer Park station for their kindness to him. Pickands Mather & Co., which operated the ship, wrote a letter of thanks to the keeper of nearby Two Hearted River station, Captain Albert Ocha, for recovering the bodies of the other crew members. This was the same Captain Ocha who was the hero of the *Robert Wallace* and *David Wallace* rescues 21 years earlier. (The cemetery at this isolated station held not only the bodies of dead seamen, but also those of Mrs. Ocha and several Ocha children.)

Exactly what happened to such a new, well-built freighter—one that should have been able to weather much heavier storms? It seemed clear enough to steamboat men of the day.

Between 12:30 and 1:00 P.M. on Friday, the *Cyprus* had passed the steamer *George Stephenson,* which was towing the barge *Magna;* the *Stephenson* had one boiler disabled and was limping along at only about four miles per hour. Captain H. G. Harbottle of the *Stephenson* estimated that the *Cyprus* was making about nine knots when she passed. He noticed that she was taking some water on deck, and that she was leaving a red wake behind in the gray lake—a sign that water was entering her hold, mixing with the red iron ore she carried and then being pumped out. Evidently, the seas breaking over her deck caused enough water to enter her hold through her hatch covers to create a slushy mixture with the ore, a mixture that shifted as the vessel rolled along during the stormy weather. By late afternoon this had produced the fatal list.

The hatch covers of the *Cyprus* were of a telescoping design common to vessels of that period; they were made of overlapping steel sections and when they were opened the sections slid back, one on top of the other, to form a neat stack at each end of the open hatch. But when they were closed the overlapping plates were not completely watertight. For that reason, tarpaulins were provided to fit over the metal covers, but the mechanism for operating the covers placed so many obstructions in the way that it was hard to fit the tarpaulins in place. Apparently for this reason, Captain Huyck did not have the tarpaulins fitted over the metal hatch covers. Or, as one contemporary writer put it, "The navigators evidently were in the habit of leaving the tarpaulin in storage and trusting to luck. In this instance luck proved a bad factor and a terrible lesson."

Top: On her second voyage the *Cyprus* was lost with all but one of her crew. Here is some of the wreckage that washed ashore. (Courtesy Center for Archival Collections, Bowling Green State University)
Bottom: The liferaft on which the one survivor from the *Cyprus* came ashore. The figure on the raft in the picture is a lifesaver, as are the other men. (Courtesy Center for Archival Collections, Bowling Green State University)

Wrecking

In the early days, salvage efforts were often very informal. Here is the Canadian steamer *Rosedale*, ashore on Knife Island, Lake Superior, in 1893. The ship was built in England and brought across the Atlantic. She was pulled off and served for many more years. As is true of many such early incidents, no written record of the incident is known. (Courtesy Kenneth Thro)

*V*arious companies were in the business of wrecking, in the sense of salvaging wrecked vessels. In earlier years it was a part-time, almost casual outgrowth of other work. One such company was the Calvin firm, based on Garden Island, near Kingston, at the foot of Lake Ontario, where the waters of the Great Lakes flow into the St. Lawrence River on their way to the sea. The Calvins (over the years from 1836 to 1914 their firm had several names: the Kingston Steam Forwarding Company; Calvin, Cook and Counter; Calvin and Cook; Calvin and Breck; Calvin and Son; and finally the Calvin Company Ltd.) were timber merchants and timber forwarders. They bought timbers throughout the Great Lakes region, brought them to Garden Island in their own vessels, made them into rafts, and sent the rafts down the St. Lawrence to the timber coves of Quebec City. There the timbers were put aboard ocean ships for England. The Calvins also transported timbers in this way for other owners, and on occasion they used their ships for other cargoes.

As their business developed they built their own vessels—schooners, steamers, river tugs—which in time met with the usual accidents. The Calvins were prepared to salvage them when necessary, and soon were asked to help with other ships that were wrecked or stranded. As early as 1851 they salvaged the little schooner *Globe*, which ran ashore near Garden Island in a December snowstorm.

One of the bitterest salvage jobs must have been that of the firm's own tug *Hercules* in 1858. The tug's boiler exploded while she was towing a disabled steamer up Rapide Plat in the St. Lawrence. Among those killed were D. D. Calvin, Jr., aged 22, who had been expected soon to take over management of the firm from his father, the founder, then past 60. The elder Calvin went to the scene, took part in recovering his son's body and superintended the raising of the *Hercules*.

Calvin vessels continued to get into trouble from time to time. On one such occasion around the turn of the century, a Calvin steamer loaded with wheat went aground in a fog on Long Point, the finger of land that reaches out into Lake Erie and has wrecked many a ship. The weather was good, but the month was October and a storm could be expected at any time. "The Boss"—H. A. Calvin, son of the senior D. D. Calvin—gave orders that, among other vessels, one of the river tugs (a boat not too seaworthy in the open lake) would go to the assistance of the stranded freighter. The tug captain demurred. He was told that *she* would go, whether *he* went or not, to which he responded unhappily, "All right sir, I know I'll be drowned, but I'll go." In telling the story, D. D. Calvin, grandson of the founder, remarked, "He went, but he died in bed long years afterward, for the fine weather held and the job was quickly and successfully done."

Usually the men of Garden Island liked wrecking. They received extra pay for it, and though the work was hard it was more exciting than their usual routine. To quote D. D. Calvin again, "I have never heard that any of our islanders followed the alleged custom of the early Scilly islanders, and actually hoped, even prayed, for wrecks. No, but they welcomed them, all the same!"

On the American side of the Lakes a number of firms, most of them owners of tugs used also for other purposes, had entered the wrecking business by the final years of the nineteenth century. But as ships grew continually larger, many of these companies were no longer able to provide adequate towing or wrecking service. In 1899 the Great Lakes Towing Company, based at Cleveland, was organized from several of the smaller firms. It soon emerged as the major operator of tugboats on the Great Lakes.

One of the companies that became part of the Towing Company was the Parker & Swain Wrecking Company, owner of the wrecking tug *Favorite,* an elderly wooden vessel that, after a long career as a passenger steamer, had been converted in 1890 for wrecking. Despite her age, she remained the best wrecker on the Lakes until she burned in 1907. That same year the Towing Company had a steel wrecking tug built

The schooner *Charles Luling* was stranded in the fall of 1890 at Manistique and pulled off the following spring. The tug is the *Elmer* of Manistique. (Courtesy Marine Historical Collection, Milwaukee Public Library)

The sidewheel steamer *Corona* aground on the Canadian side of the Niagara River about 1914. Having come across Lake Ontario from Toronto, she probably ran aground in a fog while navigating on time courses (allowing a given time for each leg of a compass course). She was released and continued in service. (Courtesy Rev. Edward J. Dowling, S.J.)

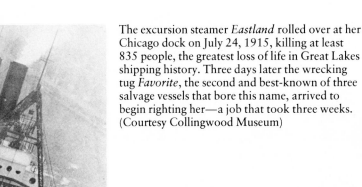

The excursion steamer *Eastland* rolled over at her Chicago dock on July 24, 1915, killing at least 835 people, the greatest loss of life in Great Lakes shipping history. Three days later the wrecking tug *Favorite*, the second and best-known of three salvage vessels that bore this name, arrived to begin righting her—a job that took three weeks. (Courtesy Collingwood Museum)

at Buffalo; she was 195 feet long and her engines provided 1200 horsepower. Also named *Favorite*, she was active on the Great Lakes until she was requisitioned in 1917, during World War I, and sent to salt water by the U.S. Shipping Board. In 1919 the Towing Company built another, slightly smaller wrecking tug to replace this one. She, too, was named *Favorite* and she lasted until 1954, when she had become so old and creaky that the company retired her. Thus, over a period of some years, the most powerful wreckers on the Lakes were named *Favorite* (usually pronounced with a long "i").

The second *Favorite* was involved in what probably were the two most complicated wrecking jobs that ever took place in these waters.

On July 24, 1915, the excursion steamer *Eastland* rolled over at her dock in the Chicago River, with the loss of at least 835 lives—the greatest disaster in all the history of Great Lakes shipping. On July 27, the *Favorite*, which had been stationed at St. Ignace, arrived to raise her. The wreckers sealed off all underwater openings in the *Eastland's* hull, then

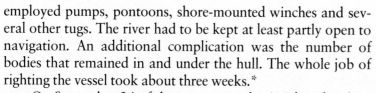

employed pumps, pontoons, shore-mounted winches and several other tugs. The river had to be kept at least partly open to navigation. An additional complication was the number of bodies that remained in and under the hull. The whole job of righting the vessel took about three weeks.*

On September 24 of that same year the 416-foot freighter *Western Star,* carrying 7,000 tons of coal through the North Channel of Lake Huron, struck Robertson's Rock, a vicious peril to navigation. Within minutes she began to sink; her crew took to the boats and escaped. Finally she lay at an extreme angle, her bow in seven feet of water and her stern in 114 feet.

The Great Lakes Towing Company received the contract to raise her. This job was far less grim than that of the *Eastland,* but it was even more difficult. During the following winter the salvagers built a coffer dam through the ice. Then they set pumps to work removing the water inside the dam. The whole structure, built of unseasoned timbers, promptly collapsed under the pressure of the water outside it.

On June 17, 1916, the *Favorite* and a fleet of lighters and smaller tugs arrived. The wreckers proceeded to build a stronger coffer dam, the foundation of which was made of heavy timbers that divers bolted to the *Western Star's* gunwales. A stout wood-and-metal framework was built up from this foundation and covered with "wrecking cloth"—heavy, waterproof canvas. While the work was progressing, a stiff northwest storm arose and waves battered the partly completed structure, damaging it so that it required considerable

*For a more complete account of the *Eastland* disaster see pages 190-93 of *Ships of The Great Lakes* by James P. Barry, Howell-North Books, 1973.

Left: The freighter *Western Star* sank in September 1915 after striking Robertson's Rock in the North Channel of Lake Huron, and lay with her bow in seven feet of water, her stern in 114 feet. This is how she looked just before the most difficult salvage job ever done on the Great Lakes was begun on her.
Above: Some of the divers employed on the *Western Star* salvage job.

Opposite: (top left) During the winter of 1915-16 salvagers constructed this coffer dam around the *Western Star,* but the dam was not strong enough and when the water was pumped out of it, it collapsed.
Top right: On June 17, 1916, after the wrecking tug *Favorite,* the lighter *T.F. Newman* and several other tugs arrived on the scene, work began on a new and stronger coffer dam. Here heavy canvas is fitted over the frame.
Center: Side view of the dam around the sunken part of the ship. Men are fitting canvas toward the right end of the dam.
Bottom left: The completed dam, as seen from the bow of the *Western Star.*
Bottom right: View in the opposite direction from one of the salvage vessels.
(All photographs, courtesy Marine Historical Collection, Milwaukee Public Library)

repair. When the dam was completed it contained 430,000 feet of timber, 150,000 pounds of metal rods and 220,000 square yards of canvas. Again pumps were put to work emptying out the water, and the vessel slowly rose. On September 18, 1917, two years after the wreck, the *Western Star* was finally towed into port.

The practice of wrecking, in the sense of luring ships to disaster in order to plunder them, seems never to have taken place on the Lakes. That of plundering them after disaster was seldom done as openly or on as grand a scale as in some other parts of the world. But human nature being what it is—and salvage laws at times permitting—many wrecks were stripped. And on occasion, valuable things washed ashore from disasters were gathered in by nearby residents.

One such wreck was that of the iron-hulled sidewheeler *Muskegon*, destroyed by a storm at the entrance to the harbor of her namesake city, Muskegon, Michigan. In a northwest gale, the vessel approached port at 4:30 in the morning of October 28, 1919. A sandbar off the harbor entrance deflected the big waves in unexpected directions; one terrible wave picked up the 1,149-ton steamer and drove her onto the south pier. Her engines stopped and all her lights went out. For 10 minutes she hung there, her starboard rail against the pier, while the crew tried to get the passengers over the rail and onto the pier. But the doors of those below in their staterooms were locked shut by the list of the ship and the

Opposite (top left): Completed coffer dam, just before the salvagers began to pump out the water. Center: As the water is pumped out of it, the dam rises, bringing the sunken hull with it. Top right: Another view of the dam rising as water is pumped out of it. Bottom left: These men are standing on the deck of the *Western Star*. Ahead of them, the coffer dam rises in the air. Bottom right: The forward end of the *Western Star* with her deck level again, as seen from one of the salvage vessels. (Entire sequence, courtesy Marine Historical Collection, Milwaukee Public Library)

By contrast, other salvage jobs were more primitive. The schooner *Rosabelle* capsized in a Lake Michigan gale on October 30, 1921, with the loss of 11 lives. The wreck floated ashore several days later at Racine, Wisconsin, and was stripped. (Courtesy Kenneth Thro)

stresses of her twisted hull, and they were forever trapped. Then the hull split and the steamer dropped into the churning water at the end of the pier. Second mate Fred Steffans clung to the pilot house, which was washed down the channel. He was eventually seen by someone and pulled out. A nearby light-house keeper and Coastguardsmen rescued others. One Coast-guardsman found two lightly clad women, both with broken ankles; he loaded them in a wheelbarrow and took them to shelter. Of the 39 passengers and 52 crew members, 31 were lost.

As daybreak came, hundreds of spectators gathered and discovered that the beach was full of wreckage for more than two miles south of the harbor entrance. Much of the ship had disintegrated into small pieces. Mixed with the wreckage people found clothing, blankets, food, candles and chairs. There was a feast of candy for the children and hundreds of pairs of silk hosiery for the women.

Those along the shore filled pockets, baskets and boxes. One resident, then a young boy, recalled that his father used some of the wood to make a plank walk behind their house, though his mother refused to use a bucket of yellow soap chips that had been washed ashore, not wanting to profit from the misfortune of others. In later years, during the Great Depression, she finally decided to use them.

Salvage work beginning on the liner *Huronic*, which went aground on Lucille Island, Lake Superior, on August 6, 1928. After being refloated, she served for many more years on the Lakes. (Courtesy Collingwood Museum)

The steamer *Muskegon* was wrecked on the south pier at the entrance to the harbor of Muskegon, Michigan, on October 28, 1919. After hanging on the pier for 10 minutes, the hull split. Wreckage washed along the piers and onto the beaches, and people brought baskets and boxes to gather up items they could use.

The machinery of the *Muskegon* standing in the water after the storm. (Both, courtesy Dossin Great Lakes Museum)

Wrecks of the Twenties and Thirties

The *City of Bangor* ashore on Keweenaw Point with her ice-covered deckload of autos. (Courtesy Hamilton Collection, Rutherford B. Hayes Library)

During the 1920s and 1930s light buoys of improved design were installed on the Great Lakes; automation of lighthouses began (though whether that was an improvement is debatable); the first icebreaking Coast Guard cutter was launched; and regular publication began of the periodical, *Notices to Mariners*. Prohibition doubled U.S. Coast Guard strength in men and small craft on the Lakes. The immediate purpose was to control smuggling, but it also improved the lifesaving capabilities of that service.

Most important was the growing use of radio. In 1925 the Huron Lightship began sending out the first radio fog signals on the Lakes. In 1937–38 six stations along the Lakes began voice radio broadcasts of notices to mariners and marine weather forecasts. Use of radio communication aboard ships increased greatly, though not until after World War II did laws actually require lake ships to carry radio.

There were not as many disasters, but wrecks continued to occur. None of the improved aids controlled the occasional bad judgments of men, and none of them controlled the weather.

The 445-foot steamer *City of Bangor* headed westward into Lake Superior after passing through the canal at Sault Ste. Marie on November 29, 1926. There had been a series of recent gales, but Captain

William J. Mackin decided to push on out into the stormy lake.

His freighter, built originally as an ore carrier, had been converted the year before to carry automobiles. Two additional decks had been built in her cargo holds to carry the cars, and other cars were loaded on the spar deck—the long, open deck of a lake freighter. Altogether she carried on this trip 248 new Chryslers. The weight of the cars did not approach that of the bulk cargoes for which she had originally been designed. As a result she rode high, presenting her flat topsides to the wind and without enough of the hull in the water to take a good bite on it.

She plodded westward over the lake, however, in the face of growing northwest winds and heavy snow. On toward Duluth she went, steering by compass. This was long before radar, and the snow blanketed any shore lights that Captain Mackin might otherwise have seen. Off Keweenaw Point the wind became so strong that it blew the ship around and into the trough of the waves. Like many lake freighters of the day she was sadly underpowered; small engines used less fuel and thus cost less to operate. She was not strong enough to fight her way out of the trough and the seas began to wash over her and carry away some of the cars lashed on deck. Then, to add to her problems, the steering engine failed. Out of control, she was driven toward the shore.

About dark on the 30th she grounded, bumping up on the shelving bottom 75 yards from shore, and the seas immediately began to wash over her. The men aboard could only stay closed up in their deckhouses and hope that she did not break apart. When she ran ashore, a large rock punched into the hull aft; water began to come in and soon drowned the fire under the engine-room boilers. There then was no heat aboard; the weather grew colder outside and ice from the breaking waves built up on the hull. In the after house the men had the coal range in the galley to warm them, but forward they were forced to chop out some of the wooden paneling and build a bonfire.

The following morning the storm subsided and the men began to chop themselves out of their ice-crusted quarters. The captain ordered them to chop free one of the lifeboats. By afternoon the lifeboat was ready and several crew members, carrying lines attached to the wreck, worked their way to shore. There they secured one line to a tree and with the other pulled the boat back and forth until everyone was ashore.

But being ashore was little better than being on the wreck. Deep snow was everywhere and there was no shelter. Many of the men wore clothing inadequate for protection from the cold. They girded themselves, however, and hiked off toward the nearest small village, Copper Harbor. They became lost,

Some of the Chryslers on deck have been cleared of ice, preparatory to being unloaded. (Courtesy Hamilton Collection, Rutherford B. Hayes Library)

spent the night in the woods around a makeshift fire, and in the morning wearily worked their way back to the wreck. There they built a fire as a beacon, hoping that it might be seen by rescuers.

That same series of storms had driven several other ships onto Keweenaw Point. Among them was the freighter *Thomas Maytham,* which on December 1 had gone on a reef on the eastern side of the point. Just as the *Bangor's* men were settling down for another cold, bleak night, around the point came a 36-foot motor lifeboat from the Coast Guard station at Eagle Harbor, carrying the crew of the *Maytham.*

Boatswain Anthony Glaza, commanding the lifeboat, surveyed the situation with understandable surprise. Then he told Captain Mackin that he would take his present load of rescued seamen, who crammed his boat to the gunwales, to Copper Harbor and return for the crew of the *Bangor.* Mackin's men only needed to keep the beacon fire burning high so that he could find them again. True to his word, he returned late that night, lifted the *Bangor's* crew to Copper Harbor, and then loaded up the *Mayham's* men again and headed off to more distant Eagle Harbor. Meanwhile the *Bangor's* people, with a couple of Coast Guardsmen left by Glaza to care for them, were billeted in a nearby farmhouse.

Several days later Glaza returned in his lifeboat. On his heels came another gale, which left his boat frozen in the ice so firmly that it remained there all winter. In due course both Coast Guardsmen and the *Bangor's* crew were taken by sleigh to the nearest railroad, by which they traveled on to their various destinations.

Through the winter months the insurance underwriters worked at chopping cars free from the deck of the *City of Bangor* and cutting holes in the side of the hull to get out the cars below decks. In February, after mobilizing the road crews of two counties to clear back roads usually left unplowed in winter, they were able to drive a procession of cars to the railroad. The ship was abandoned where she lay.

The Canadian freighter *Altadoc*, 365 feet long, bound empty from Owen Sound to Fort William on the night of December 7, 1927, met a Lake Superior storm with gusts to 70 miles per hour and blinding snow. In time the pounding seas damaged her steering gear. Helpless, she and the 25 men aboard were carried southward across the lake. About 6:10 P.M. on December 8 she drove ashore on Keweenaw Point within a thousand feet of the year-old wreck of the *City of Bangor*. Captain R. D. Simpson of the *Altadoc* did not know his location until he saw the wrecked *Bangor*. (This was the second wreck of the captain's career. Forty-two years previously he had been second mate in the *Algoma* when she was wrecked off Isle Royale.)

Captain Simpson's wrecked ship, her hull cracked in two, offered uncertain shelter in the subzero weather. So he had Chief Engineer Hardman and three seamen take a lifeboat ashore through the breakers and set out on foot to Copper Harbor for help. They plodded through heavy snow and eventually reached the town with their story—but in such condition that the people there put them in sleighs and conveyed

The *Altadoc*, her back broken, lies on Keweenaw Point a thousand feet from where the *City of Bangor* was wrecked the year before. (Courtesy Dossin Great Lakes Museum)

them to the hospital in the next town, Calumet, for treatment.

Simpson continued to send SOS radio messages. One was picked up at 4:10 P.M. on the 8th. The radio station notified the Eagle Harbor Lifeboat Station, 23.5 miles from the wreck. Coastguardsman H. R. Rogers was temporarily in charge of the station in the absence of Boatswain Anthony F. Glaza, who had been on liberty at Hancock, Michigan, and was unable to return by car because the blizzard had clogged the roads with snow. Rogers alerted his crew to leave at once in the motor surfboat and telephoned Glaza at Hancock to report what was happening.

Glaza knew that a ship aground on Keweenaw Point was probably under no immediate threat of breaking up, but that launching the surfboat through the ice would be difficult at best and that even if it were done successfully, the crew of an open boat was likely to perish in the blizzard. He told Rogers to make further inquiries by radio as to conditions aboard the *Altadoc.* Rogers learned that the crew of the ship was in no present danger. Glaza then told him to stand by till daylight; meanwhile he would try to get back to the station.

Before leaving Hancock, Boatswain Glaza telephoned Boatswain C. T. Christiansen, who was in charge of the Coast Guard cutter *Crawford,* stationed at Two Harbors, Minnesota, and asked him to come and clear the ice from Eagle Harbor so the surfboat could get away, then stand by in case the motor surfboat could not re-enter any of the harbors through the ice. Christiansen agreed that he would get the *Crawford* under way at once.

Glaza started back in the storm, first taking a streetcar to Mohawk, Michigan; then getting a ride on a county snowplow to Phoenix, Michigan; then riding in a sleigh behind a team of horses for six miles; and finally, walking through the blizzard for the last six miles. He arrived at the station at midnight.

By daylight, Glaza saw that the end of the harbor was completely jammed by ice and that the boat could not get out. He waited, but there was no sign of the *Crawford* and no indication that the wind might change and blow the ice away. Although the sea was moderating off Eagle Harbor, the blizzard continued. The ice in the harbor was spreading. Shortly after noon Glaza hired a team of horses and a sleigh, had his crew load the boat on the sleigh, and took it around the frozen bay to a point where it could be launched over the ice directly into the open lake. Still there was no *Crawford.*

The *Crawford,* proceeding the previous night through a temperature of -27°F, had had to turn back to Two Harbors when her compass froze. Boatswain Christiansen did not start her out again till 9:00 the next morning, after the compass had been thawed out and the alcohol in it replaced by some bought at a local drugstore. Even then she had considerable trouble in moving through the storm and a growing fog.

Next morning, Glaza could wait no longer. At 6:00, in the frigid dawn, he and his crew began to manhandle their boat over and through the three quarters of a mile of packed ice that fringed the lake shore. About 11:10 they reached open water. Glaza and four others in the boat headed off into the heavy seas and frequent snow squalls. They reached the *Altadoc* about 1:40 that afternoon. Glaza put two of his men aboard the wreck and took 14 members of the ship's crew in his ice-crusted boat. He then set out for the small port of Copper Harbor, where about 3:20 he managed to land the rescued men. He went back and picked up the rest of the crew with their luggage and his own two men. The wind was rising and the temperature was dropping; he put a canvas boat cover over the ship's crew to protect them. Returning to Copper Harbor at 6:20 in the dusk, he saw the searchlight of a vessel off to the westward. Coming into the harbor his boat jammed in the inch-and-a-half-thick sheet ice. The weary Coastguardsmen, all of whom by this time had partially frostbitten faces, rocked the boat, hoping to free it, but succeeded only in slopping bilge water into the carburetor and stalling the engine.

At that point the cutter *Crawford*, the vessel with the searchlight, arrived in harbor. She took aboard the members of the *Altadoc*'s crew who were in the surfboat—10 men, including the master—and the boat crew, fed them hot food and made them comfortable for the night. She docked overnight at Copper Harbor, then next morning took aboard the remainder of the *Altadoc* men, including three of the four who had walked to Copper Harbor. At 8:00 A.M. she departed for Eagle Harbor, towing the motor surfboat.

The cutter arrived at Eagle Harbor about 10:30 and had to cut her way into harbor through the ice, damaging both propellers as she did so. Her people helped all the passengers ashore. Glaza and his men wrestled the ice-covered surfboat back into the boatroom of the station; its sides had been badly cut by ice and four of its planks were stove in forward of the engine compartment on the port side.

By then the roads were open. Glaza found waiting for him James Ogle, the Duluth representative of the wrecked ship's owners, and a Metro-Goldwyn news cameraman. At 1:30 the missing member of the *Altadoc* crew, one of the four who had walked to Copper Harbor and the one who had gone on from there to send "dispatches"—presumably messages from the captain—rejoined the group. At 2:00 the *Crawford* left, taking the cameraman to the scene of the wreck. Ogle had arranged for cars to take the *Altadoc* people to Calumet, and by 5:30 the last of them had departed.

After dark on November 8, 1933, the *T. S. Christie* felt her way through blinding snow squalls toward the harbor of

Manistee, on the eastern shore of Lake Michigan. Periodically the little wooden steamer blew fog signals on her whistle. Captain Louis Strahan, First Mate Robert Laury and the freighter's watchman stood on the forward deck, wrapped in heavy clothing, listening for the Manistee harbor fog horn and peering through the snowy darkness, hoping to glimpse a harbor light.

At 8:40 P.M. the captain ordered the engine checked down so that the *Christie* just drifted along, and the mate began to cast the lead line in order to take soundings. At first the line did not reach bottom. The watchman took over the line and the captain periodically moved the ship ahead a little and then let her lose headway while the lead was cast again. About 9:00 P.M. they had their first sounding; it was eight fathoms. They were approaching shore.

They crept ahead, listening, watching and taking soundings. Shortly before 10:00 Captain Strahan halted his steamer completely and she lay there for about eight minutes while he and the mate tried to determine where they were. They could hear a locomotive on shore whistling periodically, but there was no sound from the harbor fog signal. The captain decided that they were north of the harbor entrance and began to turn the vessel southward. The leadsman called out six and a half fathoms; in a minute there was a light bump as the ship touched bottom. Immediately the captain ordered full speed astern—and she backed into another sand bar and stopped. He worked her loose, and in going ahead she stuck again. She was still afloat, but she was trapped.

Through the rest of the night the people on the *Christie* blew distress signals: four long blasts of the whistle. About 11:30 the snow subsided, those on the steamer could see the harbor lights and, to add to their frustration, the fog horn at the Manistee Light Station began to blow. (Subsequent investigation showed that it had not been blowing during the snow storm.) They also could see a dredge working in the harbor and periodically coming out to dump its dredgings. The captain of the *Christie* fired rockets and continued the distress signals on the whistle. No one took notice.

The *T. S. Christie* was one of the little lumber steamers that half a century earlier had been common on the Lakes. She had been built 48 years before, at the then-thriving lumber port of West Bay City, Michigan. Rebuilt in 1921, she had had a major overhaul during the summer of 1933. Despite her age, she was sound. She was 160 feet long and of 517 gross tons. When the lumber mills were still running, it was normal practice for such vessels to carry loads of lumber both in their holds and on their decks; the high ends of the little ships helped to secure the deck cargo. The lumber cargoes had long since gone and the *Christie* was reduced to carrying pulpwood, but it was loaded in the same way.

The *T.S. Christie* about three miles north of Manistee, on Lake Michigan. She is beginning to break up. Her people came ashore in the lifeboat in the foreground. (Courtesy Hamilton Collection, Rutherford B. Hayes Library)

There she lay, about three miles north of Manistee harbor and 2,000 feet off the beach, sounding distress signals and firing rockets. Not until 5:00 the next morning was there any response. Then a Coast Guard motor lifeboat appeared alongside. Its coxswain told Captain Strahan that a northwest storm warning had been posted and advised him to abandon the ship. The captain asked the coxswain to get the dredge or a tug to help pull the *Christie* off, for she was still afloat and he felt that with a little help he could free her. The Coast Guard boat headed back to harbor. Shortly afterward the northwest storm began, with strong winds that built up high seas; more snow also fell. Waves began to break over the vessel and to wash away part of her deck cargo.

Captain Strahan ordered the steamer's lifeboat put over the side and partially lowered. He let it hang there for some time, hoping that the Coast Guard boat would return, but it did not. Finally, about 6:00, when there was no sign of help from any source, the captain ordered the crew of 14 into the boat and they came ashore, getting soaked in the process but without serious injury. Landing at 6:15, they plodded off to the Hotel Northern in Manistee.

They landed on a Thursday morning. The storm continued to pound the *Christie*. The dredge could not survive if it ventured out in the storm and there was no other vessel there that could tow the steamer. On Saturday, at 5:00 P.M., the *Christie* began to break up. Within an hour she was totally destroyed, her wreckage washing ashore.

The whaleback steamer *Henry Cort* was launched as the *Pillsbury* in 1892, but was renamed three years later. In December 1917 she was rammed by another ship and sunk in Lake Erie. Raised the following summer, she was rebuilt during the winter and given a high raised deck unusual on a whaleback.

In November of 1934, having sailed from Chicago with a cargo of pig iron, she found herself in a southerly gale. By this time two cranes had been mounted on her deck, and their weight made her topheavy and cranky. Her relatively light load on this voyage also made her hard to handle. When she was well out on Lake Michigan, the storm seized the vessel and turned her completely around. Captain Charles E. Cox had the choice of letting her run before the storm and driving ashore or of trying to reach Muskegon harbor. He decided on Muskegon.

At 10:00 P.M. on November 30 the *Cort* approached the harbor entrance. As she did, an especially large sea picked her up and smashed her against the outside of the north breakwater, tearing out her bottom, flooding her hold and engine

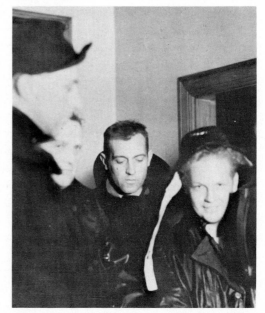

Members of the *Cort's* crew are cared for by the Coast Guard.

room, and knocking out her electrical system—thus plunging her into darkness. Other seas climbed over her and the breakwater. The Muskegon Coast Guard Station responded promptly, sending out their power surfboat. The huge waves threw the boat about so violently, however, that one man, 23-year-old Jack Dipert, was tossed out and drowned. A few minutes later the boat rolled over, throwing the remaining Coastguardsmen into the water. They managed to reach shore.

The following morning a larger power lifeboat, which had been brought in from Grand Haven, tried to reach the ship. However, it was unable to fight its way through the storm. Other Coastguardsmen, roped together as protection against the waves that still swept over the ice-clad breakwater, worked their way out the 3,000-foot distance to a point opposite the *Cort*. There they tossed a line aboard. The 60-year-old cook, Harry Sutton, was the first to come down the line, and soon all of the 25 crew members were on the breakwater rocks. Captain Cox was last ashore. The seas were subsiding, but the rock slabs of the breakwater were icy and some of the men were exhausted. The group made slow progress landward; toward the end of the trek the cook collapsed and had to be carried. The cook and the first mate—who had helped all the others leave the wreck—were taken to the hospital, where they soon recovered. The remainder were given hot coffee and dry beds.

Plans went forward to salvage the *Cort*, but less than a month after the wreck, in the early morning of December 26, a northeast gale and blizzard swept in on Muskegon and battered the ship to pieces.

The *Henry Cort* lay against the north breakwater at Muskegon as sailors were brought ashore on a line. (Both, from the Collections of the Michigan History Division)

The Recent Losses

After striking Bridge 12 in the Welland Canal at 4:20 A.M. on August 25, 1974, the ore carrier *Steelton* lies near the wrecked bridge with her bow and wheelhouse damaged. As a result of the accident, the canal was closed for two weeks while the bridge was removed from it. (Courtesy Rev. Edward J. Dowling, S.J.)

Since World War II, aids to navigation have improved vastly. The most important is undoubtedly radar, developed during that war. More recently a long-range radio navigation system, loran, has become available. The U.S. and Canadian Coast Guards have commissioned new ice breakers; marine weather forecasts have improved; air rescue capabilities have been much expanded.

All of these advances have made it safer to sail the Lakes than it used to be. We no longer have the large-scale disasters of earlier years, when one storm might cause dozens of shipwrecks. But human judgment still can err, machinery still can fail, and weather and water still are largely beyond our control. And so, the losses continue.

The narrow reaches of the rivers associated with the Lakes have dangers of their own; often they have been scenes of grounding and collision. Accidents have happened even in canals. In 1974 the freighter *Steelton*, which was passing through the Welland Canal, rammed a bridge, dropping it into the waterway. For two weeks afterward, shipping between Lakes Erie and Ontario was blocked.

The St. Lawrence is the longest river connected with the Lakes and it probably has seen the most disasters. An early one was the loss in the rapids of 64 boats

The burning *Milverton* aground following a collision in the upper St. Lawrence River. (Courtesy Hamilton Collection, Rutherford B. Hayes Library)

from the fleet of small craft that General Amherst brought down the river in 1760 to aid in the British capture of Montreal. More recently, a system of canals on the Canadian side of the river let small vessels pass by the various rapids and thus move between lake ports and the ports of the lower river and the Gulf of St. Lawrence. This system had 22 locks in 6 canals at the end of its development, just before 1959. Most of the ships passing through it were lake freighters no longer than 259 feet, the maximum permitted by the locks; these little steamers were known as "canallers." The majority were dry bulk carriers, but there were also tankers and package freighters among them.

Despite the canals, the ships continued to navigate some fast-moving parts of the river itself. Most canallers had only modest power. They were slow, and in swift waters that slowness could contribute to disaster. One such vessel was the canal-sized tanker *Translake*.

The *Milverton* was a 259-foot bulk freighter that had been built in Scotland in 1929 and brought across the Atlantic, as were many Canadian ships before World War II. About 7:00 A.M. on September 24, 1947, a clear day, she was bound downstream between Morrisburg and Iroquois, through the natural river channel. There was a strong current here in midchannel, but slack water near the shore. Downbound vessels like the *Milverton*, which were harder to control and thus

The *Milverton* aground and still smoking after being gutted by fire.

Bow view of the *Milverton* about a week after the collision. Note the blown-out bow plate at extreme left, a result of the initial explosion. Note also the swiftness of the river current. (Both, courtesy Hall Corporation of Canada and Robert Graham)

were given the right of way, stayed in the middle and rode the current; upbound ones moved through the quieter water along the shore. In this reach it was compulsory that ships pass port side to port side.

The tanker *Translake* was upbound. The *Milverton*, no doubt because of the compulsory passing rule, neglected to give the single blast of her whistle that signaled a port-side passing. As the two ships met, the *Translake* without warning sheered to port and into the path of the current-borne *Milverton*, which rammed her on the starboard side. Damage to the tanker was small and no one aboard was hurt; she went aground near the scene of the accident. But as the *Milverton* struck, there was an explosion in her forepeak—evidently from a tank of lamp oil carried there—followed quickly by a fire that spread to the wooden timbers of the forward crew's quarters and then, accompanied by still other explosions, engulfed the whole fore part of the freighter, rushing on to her highly volatile cargo of bituminous coal. The blazing vessel drifted with the current, eventually grounding on a rock.

Twelve men died, either seared in the flames, drowned after jumping overboard, or, like the second and third mates, from their burns after finally reaching the hospital. Eleven were rescued by local residents who came out to the burning ship in small boats. The wreck continued to burn for days despite efforts by salvagers to put out the fire. Eventually the hull broke in two, the stern section dropping into deeper water, while the bow remained impaled on the rock.

At the official inquiry that followed, Captain Chatel of the *Translake* contended that the strong current had caused his underpowered vessel to go off course. (Many experienced mariners felt that there could also have been a failure of the tanker's steering gear.) Captain Payne of the *Milverton* was exonerated at the hearing, receiving only the admonition that an exchange of passing signals would have been advisable.

The St. Lawrence, as Hugh MacLennan points out in his *Seven Rivers of Canada,* is an imperial river: first a river of the political empires of France and Britain, and then a river of commercial empire, linking the commerce of the Great Lakes with the sea. One small servant of that commercial empire was the steel canaller *John H. Price,* built in 1927 by Smith's Dock Co., South-Bank on-Tees, England, for the Hall Corporation of Canada, Ltd., of Montreal. She was the first ship bought by the Canadian company and she was named after a Canadian timber magnate. Of standard canal size (259 x 43.4 x 20 feet), designed to go through the small St. Lawrence locks of the day, she served many years without major incident, carrying cargo between ports on the Lakes and those on the lower St. Lawrence. On November 27, 1951, she arrived to load pulpwood at Ste. Anne des Monts, Quebec.

Ste. Anne des Monts is a small port on the lower St. Lawrence near the base of the northern shoulder of the Gaspé Peninsula, where the Rivière Ste. Anne flows into the St. Lawrence estuary. The *Price* tied up at the government dock on the east side of the river at 7:00 that morning, and by 9:15

Below: The canaller *John H. Price,* in a storm at Ste. Anne des Monts on the lower St. Lawrence, broke away from her dock and for a time lay aground parallel to it.
Opposite (series): The *Price* was swung by the wind and waves, and continued to swing until she was roughly parallel to the shore. She then was slammed against the shoal (second row, right) and her back was broken. The waves continued to pound her. Immediately after the storm (third row, right) the break in the hull amidships, the lines at the stern that were tangled in her propeller, and the lack of a rudder are evident. A view of the master's office shows the effect of the door that was stove in by the storm and a view of the pilot house shows the crew's last refuge before going ashore. (All, courtesy Hall Corporation of Canada and Robert Graham)

she began loading. Work stopped for the day at 5:00 in the afternoon; by then she had about 600 tons of wood on board. She lay with her port side against the dock, her bow pointing toward the land.

By 9:00 in the evening the wind had shifted to the northeast, growing in velocity, and snow had begun to fall. By 11:00 the wind was blowing at force 6 (a "strong breeze" of 22-27 knots). All hands were called, all moorings were put out, and the one empty ballast tank was filled. The wind continued to increase and by 3:00 next morning seas were breaking over the vessel's stern. By 4:00 the wind was at force 8 (a "fresh gale" of 34-40 knots). At that time one of the wire cables snapped and "she was ranging heavily against the wharf." Her engines were run at half astern to ease the strain on the mooring lines, but under the force of the wind the lines broke one by one.

By about 4:55 all the lines had parted and she was free from the dock. Captain Alcide Lefebvre immediately ordered both anchors dropped, but they did not hold. She went adrift, grounded briefly parallel to the dock, and then her stern swung around and she drove toward shore. At the same time, two of the trailing lines became tangled in her spinning propeller. Driven by wind and the rising tide she was forced broadside onto the reef. Her rudder carried away.

Meanwhile two other vessels in the harbor, the small Canadian goelette *Prince Mitgang* and the Norwegian *Belray*, were fighting to keep from being dashed against the dock or the shore by waves described as "mountainous."

Captain Lefebvre gathered the crew of the *Price* in his office in the forward superstructure, where they stayed until 11:45, when the force of the storm stove in the doors and flooded the room. The men moved up to the small wheelhouse and crowded into it. Heavy seas continued to break over the vessel; the rising tide carried her farther ashore and slammed her against more rocks; she filled with water and her hull buckled amidships. There was no possibility of saving her and the captain decided that the men had to get off if they could. At 3:45, during a lull in the storm, the crew worked their way aft and clustered on the wave-swept stern. They finally managed to fire a line to the wharf; it was made fast to a truck by men on shore. Starting at 5:45, the members of the crew slid ashore one by one through spray and snow in a hastily fashioned boatswain's chair, some of them disappearing momentarily under the surging waves as they went. Captain Lefebvre was the last to leave the vessel. By 6:45 all 24 hands were on solid land. Wheelsman Joachim Sauvageau made what probably was the understatement of the day: "It's good to get ashore."

The freighter was declared a total loss, but the Canadian Government required that the wreck be removed. The owners engaged Quebec Salvage and Towing to refloat her the next spring. Most of her bottom plates and much of her framing and stringers had been destroyed; her upper works had been severely battered. She was taken into the Davie Shipyard at Quebec the following May and emerged in September as an almost new ship.

The freighter *Henry Steinbrenner* left Superior, Wisconsin, at 5:11 A.M. on May 10, 1953, en route to a Lake Erie port with a cargo of 6,800 tons of iron ore. The weather was calm and clear as she moved out of harbor into Lake Superior, though the forecast called for winds up to 35 miles per hour and occasional thunder squalls.

Vessels on fresh water do not deteriorate as quickly as those on salt water, so even though she had been built in 1901, the 427-foot *Steinbrenner* was not an exceptionally old ship for the Great Lakes trade. In February 1953 she had been drydocked and inspected by the American Bureau of Shipping; the normal certificates had been issued for her. The Coast Guard had given her her annual inspection in April and had issued a clean bill of health.

Lake vessels of her vintage were fitted with telescoping hatch covers which not only had to be latched closed with clamps, but also, if they were to be completely watertight, had to be covered with tarpaulins—an additional step that often was not considered necessary during calmer months of the year. Captain Albert Stiglin had all the normal actions carried out to secure his ship for sea, but he did not have the hatches tarpaulined. (One remembers with a chill the similar decision made by Captain Huyck of the *Cyprus,* back in 1907 when such hatch covers were relatively new.)

By 4:30 that afternoon the *Steinbrenner* was steaming into heavy weather and the seas began to wash over her deck. Men were sent to check and tighten the hatch clamps, to close deadlights, and to secure chock and hawsepipe covers.

A cable lifeline ran the length of the deck of the freighter, between the forward and after superstructures, and when men ventured on deck in rough weather they fastened "traveling lines" to themselves and to rings which slid along the cable. About 8:00 in the evening, one of the leaves in the cover of the number eleven hatch worked loose. Using the traveling lines, the third mate, George L. Wiseman, and three seamen made their way aft from the forward structure in order to secure the leaf. While they were working, a big wave struck them and knocked one of the men, Thomas Wells, into the open cargo hold. The line kept him from falling more than a short distance and the others, after regaining their feet, hauled him up again. He was shaken but not seriously hurt, so they took him aft to the nearby galley and then returned and fastened the hatch-cover leaf in position. Then, feeling that they could not fight their way forward through the waves again, they, too, took shelter in the after structure.

Toward 11:00 that evening the wind velocity increased, with gusts up to 80 miles per hour, and the sea continued to build up throughout the night. By 4:30 in the morning the same hatch leaf had worked loose again, but conditions on deck were so hazardous that no one could be sent to repair it. Instead, both ballast pumps were set to pump out that hold. At about the same time, the waves broke open a door in the forward structure. Two men fastened it shut by angling planks against the door and deck and nailing them in position. An hour later the door was smashed open again, and again was secured in the same way.

The *Henry Steinbrenner* in calm weather. (Courtesy Marine Historical Collection, Milwaukee Public Library)

An illustration showing how waves wash over the deck of a freighter in heavy weather. This is the *William H. Truesdale* on Lake Erie in the 1930s. She reached port safely, presumably because her hatches were properly battened down. Similar weather (and probably bigger waves) on Lake Superior flooded the holds of the *Henry Steinbrenner* in 1953, the water entering through improperly secured hatch covers, causing the ship to founder. (Courtesy Richard J. Wright Great Lakes Marine Collection)

Captain Stigler headed the *Steinbrenner* into the wind. Seas poured on board from both sides, rushed the length of the open deck, and washed around the after house and over the fantail. At reduced speed she traveled a little more than four miles an hour. About 6:00 in the morning the movements of the ship began to grow sluggish, almost certainly from the amount of water in her holds, and toward 7:00 other hatch covers began working. The captain swung the ship hard to port under full power until she was riding stern toward the storm, hoping to put the afterdeck structure between the racing seas and the after hatch covers so that men could reach the covers and work on them; but this maneuver only permitted more seas to wash aboard. After about 10 minutes he turned her head back into the wind again. She staggered on.

Shortly past 7:00 A.M. the captain broadcast an SOS on his radio and ordered the crew to dress and put on life jackets. Half an hour later, three of the hatch covers let go completely. The captain rang the general alarm, signaled the engine room to stop the engine and made a final call on the radio for help. At that time the ship was about 15 miles due south of Isle Royale light, Lake Superior. At 7:35 the captain blew the abandon-ship signal. The 10 crew members at the forward end of the ship gathered around the life raft on the forecastle deck. Aft, in a scene of some confusion, the others began to launch the two lifeboats. Not all of the men aft wore life jackets, some having left them in various places where they now were out of reach. The group aft swung out the starboard boat, then launched it prematurely with only seven men in it. The port boat could not be swung out. Later accounts conflicted as to why this was so, but in part it seems to be because the ship was listing in the opposite direction and in part because the men were in panic. As a last resort, the boat was unhooked from its falls, so that it would float free as the ship went down.

With her cargo holds flooded, the *Steinbrenner* sank quickly. The boiling, roaring gray world swallowed her. The men forward were washed away from the raft as the ship went under; but once in the water, six of them managed to climb on it. Aft, two men were working on the port boat when the ship sank. One of them was thrown out of it; another was thrown across the boat and injured, but remained in it. Apparently at this time the boat was punctured in some way; but it floated, and two other men were able to clamber into it. Afterward it was found to have a vertical gash a little over a foot long in one side.

Alerted by the distress calls, other steamers in the area were on the lookout for survivors. The 714-foot *Joseph H. Thompson*—at that time the largest ship on the Lakes—was eastbound like the *Steinbrenner*. She found the life raft and the six men on it. The *D. M. Clemson*, also heading east, picked

A raft carrying survivors from the *Henry Steinbrenner* as seen from the rescuing steamer *Joseph H. Thompson*. (Courtesy Center for Archival Collections, Bowling Green State University)

up one of the boats and its occupants; the *Wilfred Sykes*, traveling westward, picked up the other boat and the men in it.

The *Henry Steinbrenner* sank because her cargo holds filled with water. They filled because the waves that washed over her deck loosened and finally battered open the telescoping hatch covers and poured through the hatches. The Coast Guard investigation that followed concluded that if tarpaulins had been secured over the hatch covers, the ship "in all probability would not have foundered." The lesson taught by the loss of the *Cyprus* nearly 50 years earlier had not been heeded, and as a result the ship and 17 members of her crew were lost.

The West German motor vessel *Nordmeer* was heading up Lake Huron shortly after 8:00 P.M. on November 19, 1966; the weather was clear and the 14 knot wind from the north produced seas only a foot high. Aboard the *Nordmeer* was Canadian Great Lakes pilot J. L. McGowan. The bridge watch consisted of Chief Mate Karl Wolfgang Kerlen and the wheelsman. When Kerlen came on watch at 8:00, the ship's master, Captain Steinbeck, and McGowan were on the bridge. A radar fix at 8:00 P.M. located the position of the ship. On McGowan's advice, Captain Steinbeck ordered a course that would bring the ship more nearly on the usual steamer track, and Kerlen set the change on the automatic pilot. About 8:15 the master left the bridge with the understanding that the course would be changed again after the vessel had passed the buoy on Thunder Bay Island shoal.

The West German ship *Nordmeer* aground on a reef in Lake Huron and beginning to break up. (Courtesy Hamilton Collection, Rutherford B. Hayes Museum)

About 8:20 the ship passed Thunder Bay Island to port and at the same time overhauled the lake freighter *Samuel Mather,* which was about half a mile to starboard. To avoid crossing ahead of the *Mather*, the pilot advised a change of course, which the mate applied to the automatic pilot. After three or four minutes the pilot recommended resuming the usual course taken while passing the shoal, and again the mate applied the change. Soon they passed the buoy and McGowan gave a change of course to 324 degrees true, the heading the captain had ordered. He then left the bridge, leaving instructions to call him later.

Kerlen applied the change in course to the auto pilot, evidently rather suddenly. The ship was moving at her full speed of about 14 knots; she swung to port, being carried momentarily beyond the intended course as the result of her speed and the abruptness of the change. Two minutes later she struck the reef on her port side and bounced along for several seconds before coming to a stop. Kerlen stopped the engine and sounded the general alarm. Air could be heard rushing out of the double bottom and out of the cargo hold vents on deck, and the hatches of two of the cargo holds burst open.

The feeling of those aboard on hearing a ship take the ground has been described by Joseph Conrad. "It is a sound, for its size, far more terrific to your soul than that of a world coming violently to an end." For, as he says, "the only mission of a seaman's calling is to keep ships' keels off the ground."

The captain and the pilot arrived on the bridge immediately. McGowan called the *Samuel Mather* by radio telephone and asked her to stand by, while Steinbeck and Kerlen fired red distress flares. Within five minutes the engine room was flooded. About 9:00 P.M. the *Nordmeer's* lifeboats were launched and most of the crew were transferred to the *Mather*. The captain (no doubt tasting the bitter "flavor in the mouth" that Conrad says follows such an event), two mates, the chief engineer, boatswain and carpenter remained aboard the wrecked *Nordmeer*.

About 6:20 next morning the U.S. Coast Guard cutter *Mackinaw* arrived on the scene and took aboard the men who had sheltered on the *Mather;* the lake freighter proceeded on her way. The master and seven crew members remained on the *Nordmeer.* The Coastguardsmen put out temporary navigational lights to mark the wreck.

During the following days the eight men remained aboard the stranded vessel while efforts were made to salvage her and her cargo, but on November 29 the wreck began to break up in heavy seas. Captain Steinbeck sent out a distress signal and all eight were removed successfully by Coast Guard helicopter. On December 1, 1966, the owners of the vessel—through their American agents—officially abandoned the hull.

The Coast Guard investigation put primary blame for the wreck on "the mate's incautious course change of 17 degrees toward the shoals on the left abruptly applied to the automatic pilot with the vessel making full speed through the water, causing the heading of the vessel to slew past the intended course."

*L*ake Huron is joined to Lake Erie by a heavily traveled waterway consisting of the St. Clair River, Lake St. Clair and the Detroit River. The waterway also forms the boundary here between the United States and Canada. Soon after midnight on June 5, 1972, the Canadian lake steamer *Parker Evans* neared the foot of Lake Huron. She was downbound, carrying a cargo of grain from Thunder Bay on Lake Superior. At 1:30 A.M. she entered the approaches to the St. Clair River and reduced speed to about nine miles per hour in conformity with the limits there. The night was dark but clear, with unlimited visibility.

At that time the self-unloading U.S. steamer *Sidney E. Smith, Jr.,* with a partial load of coal, was upbound in the river, approaching the lake. Both vessels displayed the proper lights. They exchanged single whistle blasts, signaling that they would pass port side to port side. As the two ships came closer, Captain Thomas Davis of the *Evans* noticed that the *Smith* did not seem to be making the normal turn into Lake Huron and he ordered his helmsman to ease off to starboard in order to give the other vessel more room.

In the wheelhouse of the *Sidney E. Smith, Jr.,* Second Mate Henry Gaskins was on watch. The captain, Arn Kristensen, had momentarily gone below to his quarters. The ship was pushing upriver against the current at her full speed of about nine miles per hour. She started a slow turn to starboard to enter the lake. Gaskins, feeling that his ship was getting too near the river bank, ordered his helmsman to reduce the amount of turn to starboard, going from about 25 degrees right rudder to about 20 degrees. Shortly afterward the *Smith* failed completely to respond to her wheel. She had moved out of the slow current near the shore to the strong current running from the lake. Her bow sagged downstream and she headed toward the American side, across the bow of the *Evans*. Gaskins saw the red and green sidelights of the *Evans* coming directly at him. He blew the danger signal and then, hastily, two blasts to signal a starboard-to-starboard passing.

Captain Davis on the *Evans* rang his engines full astern, but his ship's momentum and the current carried the *Evans* forward into the starboard bow of the *Smith*. The *Evans* rebounded and struck the other ship again some 30 feet astern of the first point of impact. Realizing the damage that must have resulted from these blows, Davis sent his ship full speed ahead in an attempt to hold the *Smith* against a nearby cement dock, but the current swung the vessel so that the maneuver did not work. The *Evans* dropped anchor and managed to get lines to a dock on shore.

Bow of the S.S. *Parker Evans* after colliding with the S.S. *Sidney E. Smith, Jr.*, in the St. Clair River about 1:30 A.M. on June 5, 1972.

Gaskins on the *Smith* rang the general alarm a few seconds before the collision. Captain Kristensen quickly returned to the pilot house, tried unsuccessfully to call the Coast Guard by radio, put the engine half ahead, and then, because of a rapidly developing starboard list, gave the order to abandon ship. Despite frantic efforts to anchor and tie her to the dock, the vessel began to drift downriver.

Meanwhile, Captain Campbell of the Port Huron–Sarnia pilot boat had been in the pilot office on the Canadian shore and had heard the whistles and the sound of impact. He called his deckhand and they quickly headed the pilot boat out to assist. Campbell got the boat into the narrow space between the *Smith* and a dock along the shore and managed to get 31 of the 34-man crew aboard the boat. At first Captain Kristensen wanted the pilot to search further for the missing men, but it was soon apparent that they had launched the ship's work skiff and had taken themselves safely ashore. The *Sidney E. Smith, Jr.* drifted into the main channel and sank, starboard side down.

Several American and Canadian agencies immediately set about recovering the oil on the *Smith* to prevent pollution. The sunken vessel now blocked one of the busiest arteries of the Great Lakes system. The U.S. Coast Guard set up traffic control, allowing northbound ships to use the channel at night and southbound ones to use it by day. Shipping in both directions was held up by the bottleneck.

The swift current undermined the wreck so that it sank further into the river bed, rolling over as it did so. The river bed was soon cut away entirely under the forward end of the *Smith,* and as a result the bow section broke off. Now, in effect, there were two wrecks.

In this situation the Navy Salvage Group in Washington D.C., which was coordinating the salvage effort, called in a Philadelphia firm, Lucker Manufacturing Company, to pro-

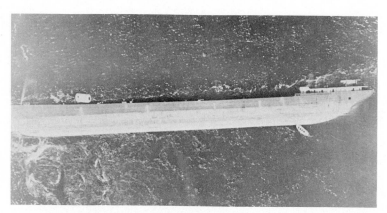

The *Smith* wreck as seen from the air. (Courtesy Center for Archival Collections, Bowling Green State University)

Hull of the *Smith* starts to shift and break in two.

The *Smith* broken in two, June 10, 1972. (Both, courtesy of the photographers, Paul A. Michaels & Son)

Cable-pulling machine attached to stern section of the *Smith*. (Courtesy Center for Archival Collections, Bowling Green State University)

vide hydraulic machines designed to pull wire rope. The Lucker firm had to have many of the parts specially made to exact specifications and shipped to it by air, but it was able to provide the completed machines to the Navy in three weeks.

In the meantime, concrete anchors had been put in place along the river bank opposite the wreck. Four of the hydraulic pulling machines, each of 80,000-pound working load, were fastened to these anchors and attached to one-and-five-eighth-inch wire ropes, the other ends of which were fastened to the stern section of the *Smith*—the major part of the vessel. Two larger machines were placed so that they held the much smaller bow section from moving and further blocking traffic. Sponge plastic was pumped into the hull to provide some buoyancy. The four machines attached to it were then started, and on June 30, in 57 minutes, they pulled it to the river bank. The channel was now largely clear.

The hull was pumped dry and left along the shore until it was later moved to be used as a dock foundation. Subsequently, the machines fastened to the bow section also drew it ashore.

Ocean ships venturing into the Great Lakes seem unusually susceptible to accident. Of course, they must operate under conditions different from those to which their crews are accustomed, moving in narrower waters and through connecting rivers, but that is not the whole story. They have had collisions and groundings here under conditions that might be met in any ocean. Sometimes the results are merely the nautical

Left: Stern section of the *Sidney E. Smith, Jr.,* being righted and raised, June 30, 1972. (Courtesy of the photographers, Paul A. Michaels & Son)
Right: Bow section of the *Sidney E. Smith, Jr.,* being righted and raised, October 8, 1972. (Courtesy of the photographers, Paul A. Michaels & Son)

equivalent of automobile fender-benders, but they are no less illustrative of the point.

On the calm, gray evening of October 2, 1973, with fog limiting visibility to half a mile or less, the Norwegian motor vessel *Rolwi* headed north in Lake Michigan at a speed of 15 knots, outward bound from Chicago. In her pilot house were the helmsman, first mate Per Bjoland, and experienced Great Lakes pilot Blair Cook. In these open waters Cook was not required to be on duty, but since he was on the bridge he was in charge of navigation.

Southward bound through the fog, heading toward Chicago, was the Liberian-registered steamship *Marathonian*, traveling at about 11.5 knots. Ahead of her, sailing the same course but moving about two knots faster, was the Greek motor vessel *Anthony*. All of these ships were visible to each other on radar. About 7:10 the *Rolwi* passed the *Anthony*, starboard to starboard. In the pilot house of the *Marathonian* Chief Mate Barbagianis noted this maneuver on his radar. With him was his helmsman; his pilot had gone below to his cabin.

After passing the *Anthony,* Cook changed course slightly to the right and called the *Marathonian* on the radio telephone. He talked to Barbagianis for a moment and then said he would meet him on "the one-whistle side" (the port side). Barbagianis, presumably still thinking of the way the two vessels had just passed, changed from a course of 240 degrees to one of 235 degrees—a move in the other direction. He afterward contended that he had so notified Cook and that Cook had answered "OK." Cook denied that any information on courses was given.

At 7:15 the *Rolwi* lost the *Marathonian* on her radar. The mate worked to adjust the radar while Cook went out on the

Opposite: Ocean ships seem especially susceptible to accident in the Lakes. The North German Lloyd M/V *Emsstein* collided with the much larger Liberian-flag M/V *Olympic Pearl*, owned by an Aristotle Onassis subsidiary, on the clear night of October 6, 1966, in a straight length of the St. Clair River. The *Emsstein* caught fire. Boats of the U. S. Coast Guard, Michigan State Police and Royal Canadian Mounted Police took off her 31 crew members, while three U. S. Coast Guard fireboats and a Canadian firefighting tug poured water on the ship. The *Olympic Pearl* was relatively undamaged. (Both photos courtesy of the photographers, Paul A. Michaels & Son)

The Norwegian M/V *Rolwi* collided with the Liberian-registered S.S. *Marathonian* in a fog on Lake Michigan on October 2, 1973. Temporary repairs were made to *Rolwi's* bow to allow her to proceed to a Montreal shipyard. Here she passes through the Welland Canal. (Photo by Ben Christensen, courtesy the *St. Catherines Standard* and E. B. Gillham)

The Greek ocean freighter *Orient Trader*, burning in Toronto harbor on July 21, 1965. Fire broke out while whe was at her pier. She was towed into open water and then beached. No lives were lost, but the ship was a total loss. (Courtesy Rev. Edward J. Dowling, S.J.)

The British freighter *Montrose* collided with a cement barge in the Detroit River on July 30, 1962, sinking near the Ambassador Bridge linking Detroit with Windsor, Ontario. (From the Collections of the Michigan History Division)

port bridge wing, peered into the gray curtain and blew the fog signal. There was no response. He blew the signal again. Meanwhile Barbagianis, on the starboard bridge wing of the *Marathonian,* heard through the fog a whistle off his starboard bow. He went into the pilot house and changed his radar from the eight-mile scale to the four-mile scale, then returned to the bridge wing and heard a ship's whistle close aboard to starboard. Neither vessel changed speed or course.

Just before 7:20 the master of the *Rolwi* arrived on the bridge at the moment that the *Marathonian's* bow loomed out of the fog, two ship lengths ahead and slightly to port. Both vessels rang their engines to "stop" but did not reverse them; each tried to steer clear of the other. They collided at 7:20, fell back slightly, and then the *Marathonian* drifted down the port side of the *Rolwi.*

Fortunately, there were no injuries. About thirty feet of plates were destroyed in the bow of each ship. The cost of repairs to the *Marathonian* totaled about $680,000; those to the *Rolwi,* $800,000.

At noon on November 10, 1975, two lake freighters slogged southeastward along the Canadian shore of Lake Superior, a northwest gale behind them. They were the *Arthur M. Anderson,* and a few miles ahead of her, the *Edmund Fitzgerald.* Both were carrying iron ore from the western end of Lake Superior; both were bound to the locks at Sault Ste. Marie and thence to unloading ports on the lower Great Lakes. Although they were American ships, and would normally have taken the shorter course along the southern shore of the lake, they followed instead the longer route in order to stay as much as possible in the lee of the northern shore—hoping to gain some protection from the growing storm.

The No. 2 lifeboat of the *Fitzgerald,* recovered along the Ontario shore after the disaster, shows the violence with which it was ripped from the ship. (Courtesy U.S. Coast Guard)

The two vessels had fallen in with each other off the Minnesota coast the preceding afternoon when the *Fitzgerald* overhauled the *Anderson*. The barometer was falling and both had received gale warnings. Captain Jesse B. Cooper of the *Anderson* and Captain Ernest McSorley of the *Fitzgerald*, talking together a little later on the radio telephone, both decided to take the northern route. The *Fitzgerald*, a somewhat faster ship, gradually pulled ahead of the *Anderson*.

On the afternoon of the 10th, about 1:40, the two captains again discussed the weather by radio. At that time McSorley commented that his ship was "rolling some." About 2:45 Cooper changed course to be certain that the *Anderson* would avoid Six Fathom Shoal near Caribou Island. Watching the *Fitzgerald* on radar—by this time visibility was nil, with heavy snow and winds up to 42 knots—Cooper felt she had gone closer to the shoal than he wanted his vessel to go. By 3:20 the wind was blowing at a steady 43 knots and the *Anderson's* deck was awash.

At about 3:30 the *Fitzgerald* called the *Anderson*. McSorley said he had "a fence rail down, two vents lost or damaged, and a list." He also said he was slowing down so that the *Anderson* could catch up—the first indication he might need help. He added that he had two of his six pumps going.

Some time later McSorley on the *Fitzgerald* had a radio conversation with the pilot of the Swedish ocean freighter *Avafors* about the radio beacon on Whitefish Point, which was not functioning. At that time the pilot heard him say to someone, "Don't allow nobody on deck!" He told the *Avafors* pilot that he had a bad list, that both of his radars were out of order, and that he was taking heavy waves over the deck in one of the worst seas he ever had been in.

Several times that afternoon the *Anderson* gave the radarless *Fitzgerald* her position. Shortly after 7:00 P.M. the *Anderson* called the *Fitzgerald* to warn her of another vessel seen approaching on radar, but to say also that that vessel would pass west of the *Fitzgerald*. When asked how they were making out with their problems, the *Fitzgerald* replied that they were holding their own.

Captain Cooper, who had been out of the *Anderson's* wheelhouse for a time, came back just as his first mate completed this conversation. Looking at the radar, he noted that the *Fitzgerald* was nine miles ahead of his ship and a little over a mile to the east. The snow had stopped and those in the wheelhouse saw the lights of approaching ships some 17 miles ahead (they were three west-bound ocean ships including the *Avafors*). The *Fitzgerald's* lights should have been closer than that, but they were nowhere to be seen; possibly she had had a power blackout. Cooper moved to the radar again. It picked up only the three distant ships. He went to the radio and called the *Fitzgerald*. There was no answer.

The *Edmund Fitzgerald* had disappeared.

After the *Anderson* gave the alarm, the three upbound ships refused to turn and join in the search, saying that it would be too dangerous in the storm. The *William Clay Ford,* a lake freighter lying in shelter in Whitefish Bay, came out into the tumult to work with the *Anderson,* searching through the night and into the next day. The Canadian lake freighter *Hilda Marjanne* also started out, but was driven back to shelter by the storm. No other ship would leave harbor until after the storm had subsided. The nearest Coast Guard cutter, the *Naugatuck,* lying at Sault Ste. Marie, suffered an oil line failure and could not get under way until next morning. But a more efficient search would have accomplished little.

A few items from the *Fitzgerald* were later found afloat or along the shore: a fragment of one lifeboat and all of the badly mangled second lifeboat, both apparently torn loose when the ship sank; one life raft floating in the lake and one on the rocks along the Ontario shore, both having inflated automatically; unused life preservers; and an assortment of other oddments that had floated off the deck or been torn loose from it. No bodies were recovered.

In due course the wreckage of the ship was located on the bottom. She had broken in two, the bow section remaining upright in the mud, the stern section 170 feet away and upside down. It was generally agreed that she had probably dived suddenly, struck the bottom, and cracked in two; and that her dive occurred because, unknown to the captain, she had taken in far more water than could have resulted from the fairly light damage he reported, or than he could have suspected when he used only two of his six pumps.

The U.S. Coast Guard Marine Board of Investigation, while noting that the exact cause of the disaster could not be determined (the ship was in such deep water that although photos could be taken of her, divers could not get down to her), stated that the most probable cause was massive flooding of the cargo hold because the hatch covers were ineffectively fastened; that the heavy seas rolling over the spar deck had poured into the holds; and that the ship had gradually lost buoyancy and stability until she suddenly plunged under. The board pointed out it was known there had been some earlier damage to the hatches caused by dockside unloading equipment and that it had not been repaired. Judging by the underwater photographs of the wreck, many of the hatch-cover clamps were loose instead of being securely dogged. (The *Fitzgerald* had solid hatch covers far superior to those that caused the losses of the *Cyprus* and *Steinbrenner*—assuming that her equipment was in good condition and everything was properly fastened.)

The board also pointed out that, under regulations established in 1973, the winter load line assigned the *Fitzgerald*

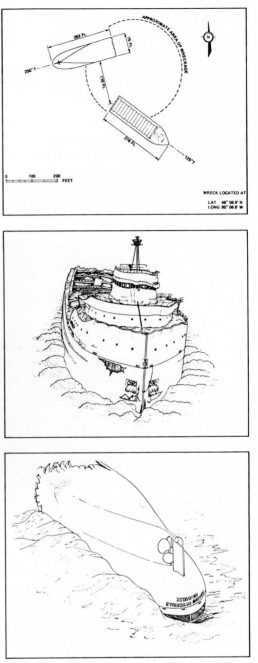

The Coast Guard underwater survey showed the positions of the bow section of the *Fitzgerald* and of the upside-down stern section on the bottom of Lake Superior. Sketches of the battered bow section and the capsized stern section were drawn from the underwater survey photographs. (All, courtesy U.S. Coast Guard)

permitted her to be loaded more than three feet deeper than was allowed when she was launched in 1958, thus reducing her buoyancy and permitting seas to wash her deck more freely. Further, there was no system for sounding the depth of water in the hold, so the captain could not realize what was happening. And finally, the transverse bulkheads were not watertight, so the water in the hold could move freely throughout its length. The Coast Guard board recommended changes in ship construction and operational procedures to correct these matters in the future.

The Lake Carriers' Association, faced with this indictment of common shipping practices on the Lakes and with the expense to shipowners of carrying out the recommendations, defended the shipping industry, writing that it "completely rejected the Coast Guard theoretical cause of the *Fitzgerald* sinking," and going on to say," when changes running into millions of dollars are recommended based only on a *possible* cause of an accident, industry most vigorously objects."

The Association gave an alternative theory. It reviewed the events before the *Fitzgerald* loss, emphasizing that "minutes after passing Six Fathom Shoal" the *Fitzgerald* reported a list, and stating that the only reasonable conclusion was that the vessel had been holed while passing the shoal, but that because the water was so rough and she was being pounded so hard, her master did not realize what had happened. The Association also pointed out that since the disaster, the Canadian government had resurveyed Six Fathom Shoal and that an unrecorded shoal *less* than six fathoms deep had been discovered more than a mile east of it.

The U.S. National Transportation Safety Board, however, reviewed the findings and on May 4, 1978, reached a conclusion similar to that of the Coast Guard, though differing from it in some ways. This board concluded that topside damage and hatch covers that were not watertight allowed partial flooding of the ship, causing her to ride progressively lower in the water and to develop the list. This in turn led her to take greater quantities of water across her decks, and the weight of the water eventually caused one or more hatch covers to collapse, permitting the waves to pour into her hold and send her to the bottom.

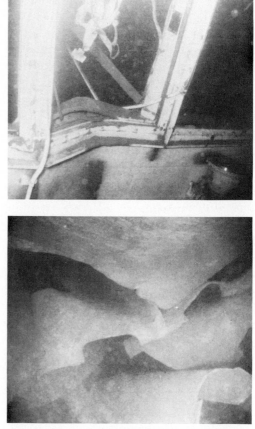

Top: Underwater photograph (taken at 590 feet) of the *Fitzgerald* wheelhouse.
Bottom: Underwater photo of the curled steel plates at the broken end of the stern section, indicating the force with which the ship was torn in two.
Opposite: The vessel's name on her stern, shown in underwater photographs. (All *Fitzgerald* pictures, courtesy U. S. Coast Guard)

𝒯he 480-foot-long, 17-year-old British ocean freighter *Photinia* came to Milwaukee harbor empty, to load grain. On Friday, May 12, 1978, she was inspected to make certain her hold was clean and ready. Then she moved outside the harbor breakwater and anchored among several other ships to wait her turn for loading.

The weather quickly became worse. By 3:30 the

following morning the *Photinia* began to drag her anchor; at 4:00 Captain Austin Patrick Collins decided to take her out into the open lake for safety. She was on her port anchor; shortly before 5:00 A.M. he ordered the winch started to weigh the anchor. He also rang for the engine to go ahead. At that time the ship was drifting backward at an average of 30 feet per minute.

Although she was propelled by a diesel engine, all of the vessel's auxiliary engines were driven by steam from a central boiler in the engine room. The engineer on watch was unable to keep pressure in the boiler, which provided power for both the anchor winches and the steering engine. When the anchor chain was partly in, he called the captain and asked him either to reanchor or to secure the anchor windlass until the boiler fuel system could be repaired. Captain Collins rang the signal to stop the main engine and shortly after 5:40 he told the chief engineer, who by then had arrived in the engine room, to proceed with the repairs. At the same time he had the port anchor chain slackened again.

The ship was still being driven before the storm, so at 5:52 the captain let go the starboard anchor—and then realized that in doing so he had perhaps crossed the two anchor chains. The wind now was blowing from the northeast at 50 knots and was producing 15-foot waves; in addition there was rain and fog. Just before 6:00 the captain called the Coast Guard to request a tug to help the *Photinia*. The Coast Guard had no tugs in the area, but referred him to two commercial tugs stationed in the harbor. He was unable to reach either of them by radio.

At 7:00 the engineers reported to the bridge that they could provide steam again. Captain Collins asked that they notify him as soon as they were able to get the main engine ready for operation. At 7:20 they signaled that the main engine was ready and the captain went ahead at one-eighth speed. At the same time he started the winches to bring in both anchors. By now the *Photinia* was dragging her anchors and moving downwind at a rate of 80 feet per minute. Shortly after 7:30, the men at the bow winches reported that the anchor chains were crossed and wound around each other; it was impossible to winch them in any farther.

By this time the ship was dragging at more than 100 feet per minute in a southerly direction, generally parallel to the shore line but gradually moving into shallower water. The gale-force winds striking against the high, light vessel, which was tethered to two useless anchors, caused her to swing about so violently that at one moment the anchor chains were stretched out dead ahead, at another they were four points off the starboard bow, and at still another they were two points abaft the beam on the port side.

At 8:00 Captain Collins sent a "Mayday" call, the voice

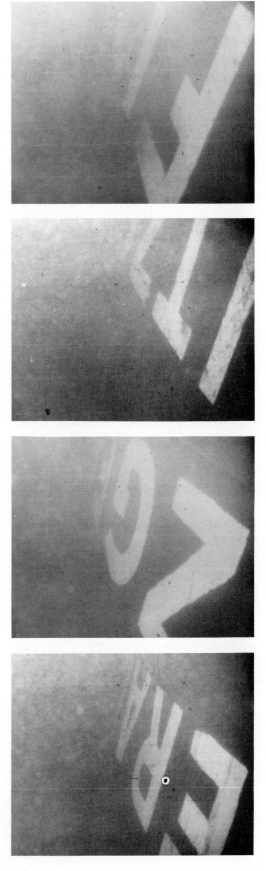

radio equivalent of an SOS, to the Coast Guard. At this time the ship's gangway, about 30 feet above the water, was damaged by the seas that were striking it. From then until 12:51 P.M., the captain slackened his anchor chains and tried various maneuvers—but during this time the *Photinia* was carried another 1,900 feet into shoal water. The wind blew at between 48 and 55 knots. Finally the ship lodged on the bottom, 500 yards off shore and about five miles from her original anchorage.

She lay on the bottom, rolling and pounding against it in the waves. She might either break up or roll over. The captain asked the Coast Guard to take the crew off the ship. A Coast Guard helicopter piloted by Lieutenant Commander Dennis Robbins had flown in from Chicago in response to the emergency call that morning. The helicopter has replaced the breeches buoy—which is no longer used—and in many cases, the surfboat. At 1:35 Robbins began to evacuate the crew.

The ship was lodged in shoal water with her stern pointing northeast, into the wind, and her bow closer to land. The only place from which men could be taken off by helicopter was a small patch of deck at the very stern. But for Robbins to hover there, he had to keep the nose of his aircraft pointed into the wind, and this put him in a position where he was unable to see the ship. In order to see anything, he had to twist his head around at an extreme angle, quickly causing a crick in his neck.

The helicopter had a three-man crew: Robbins, his copilot, and an enlisted crewman. The copilot handled the radios and watched the instruments. The crewman, Christian Carlsen, stood inside the big side door of the aircraft and operated the winch that controlled the cable hanging from a short arm on the side of the helicopter. He talked by intercom to Robbins, directing him in his flying so that the rescue basket on the end of the cable reached the small target of the deck. The helicopter, buffeted by the gusty wind, was in a "high hover" at 60 to 70 feet—a difficult position to maintain, and a dangerous one, for if the engine had failed coming down safely would have been almost impossible.

The aircraft drew up one man at a time. When it had two on board it carried them to a small field near the edge of the water, landed, and let them jump out. Then it returned to get two more and repeated the process. After it had used up some fuel, thus reducing the weight it carried, the flyers were able to bring up three men before taking them ashore. During this time the wind lessened somewhat and the flying became easier. When only "seven or ten" men were left aboard the ship, the helicopter crew stopped to refuel at a tank truck brought down to the shore from the Milwaukee commercial airfield. Robbins then took over the copilot seat; the copilot flew the aircraft

A Coast Guard helicopter rescues crew members from the British freighter *Photinia*, stranded off Milwaukee on May 13, 1978. The ship was abandoned. In rescues today the helicopter has replaced the breeches buoy, which is no longer used, and in many cases even the surfboat. (Courtesy *Milwaukee Journal*)

and they took off the remainder of the crew. The captain was the last one off and the rescue was ended soon after 4:30. By then there were several holes in the bottom of the ship and 12 feet of water had entered her engine room.

The full extent of damage to the bottom of the ship could not be determined. Her rudder, propeller and stern frame were also damaged. Her owners, Stag Line Ltd. of Northumberland, England, decided a week later to abandon her to the underwriters. She was bought by a salvage company that took 36 days to free her, working during the following June and July. She then was towed to Sturgeon Bay, but after attempts to repair her there were unsuccessful, was subsequently taken to Lake Calumet, Illinois. In the fall of 1979 she was towed to Kewaunee, Wisconsin, for scrapping.

Several months after the rescue, Robbins and Carlsen were awarded medals for their part in it.

Conclusion

Remains of the *Maplehurst*, the ship on which 10 crew members and the captain died after refusing to get into a Coast Guard motor lifeboat. (Courtesy Dossin Great Lakes Museum)

A feeling of high tragedy seems to grow almost unconsciously among those aboard as a vessel nears her end. Every ship has her own personality and it is a poor tub whose people have no pride in her. The affection of sailors for what seems a living object long ago led them to think of ships as feminine beings. More than one master has elected to die with his steel mistress rather than escape to safety with the crew. And in one astounding instance—that of the Canadian freighter *Maplehurst,* lost on Lake Superior in November 1922—10 members of her crew refused to get into a Coast Guard motor lifeboat and instead went down with their captain and ship.

The fascination of shipwreck is partly that of any disaster, in which we say to ourselves, "There but for the grace of God go I," but it is even more. In life we simultaneously love and fear the natural forces that bring both sustenance and death; a shipwreck brings home how near to us they are in the large bodies of water of the world, where in summer children play and in winter sailors drown. A wreck is high tragedy in which, like Hamlet or Macbeth, men may be brought down by forces beyond their control. Our mariners, our ships, have pitted themselves against raw power and have been overwhelmed.

Bibliography and Notes

List of Abbreviations Used

ARUSLSS	*Annual Report of the United States Life Saving Service*
IS	*Inland Seas*
LLC	*Lake Log Chips*
MR	*Marine Review*
PAC	Public Archives of Canada
T	*Telescope*
USCG	United States Coast Guard
USNA	United States National Archives

Chapter 1

For information on the *Frontenac* see George A. Cuthbertson, *Freshwater* (Toronto: Macmillan of Canada, 1931).

The following references concerning the loss of the *Ontario* are in PAC, MG-21, in the volumes shown. General Haldemand to Lord George Germain, Nov. 20, 1780, Vol. B-55. Captain Alex Fraser to General Haldemand, Nov. 18, 1780, Vol. B-100. General H. W. Powell to General Haldemand, Nov. 18, 1780, Vol. B-100. Guy Johnson to General Haldemand, Nov. 18, 1780, Vol. B-107. Captain Alex Fraser to Captain Methews, Nov. 15, 1780, Vol. B-127. Captain Alex Fraser to General Haldemand, Nov. 29, 1780, Vol. B-127. Also in the PAC, RG 8, "C" Series, Vol. 722-A, is "A General Return of His Majesty's Armed Vessels on Lake Ontario," January 1779, which gives particulars on the *Ontario*.

For reproductions of some early ship and harbor photographs see James P. Barry, *Ships of the Great Lakes* (Berkeley: Howell-North, 1973).

The comparative wreck figures were given by Richard T. Race, hydrographer and salvage specialist, in a talk to the Great Lakes Historical Society on May 20, 1978.

Information about the "Big Blow" of November 1913 may be found in Frank Barcus, *Freshwater Fury* (Detroit: Wayne State University Press, 1960); Dwight Boyer, *True Tales of the Great Lakes* (New York: Dodd, Mead & Company, 1971); and Captain Robert A. Sinclair, *Winds Over Lake Huron* (Hicksville, N.Y.: Exposition Press, 1977). The quotation from Captain Hagen is in the Barcus book.

The storm of 1905 is described by Dr. Julius F. Wolff, Jr., "Grim November," *IS* Vol. 18 (1962).

References on the loss of the *Fitzgerald* include the following (see also the references for the more detailed account of her loss in chapter 6): *Newsweek*, Nov. 24, 1975. *LLC*, Nov. 13 and 30, 1975; Oct. 9, 1977. *Seaway Review*, Autumn 1977.

Information about the *George M. Cox* appears in Dana Thomas Bowen, *Shipwrecks of the Lakes* (Daytona Beach, Fla.: privately published, 1952); Frederick Stonehouse, *Isle Royale Shipwrecks* (Marquette, Mich.: Harboredge Press, 1974); and Dr. Julius F. Wolff Jr., "A Lake Superior Lifesaver Reminisces," *IS* Vol. 24 (1968). The Rev. Edward J. Dowling, S. J., provided additional information about the wreck.

Basic references about lifesaving on the Lakes are as follows. Commander Robert Frank Bennett, USCG, "The Life-Savers: 'For Those in Peril on the Sea,'" *U.S. Naval Institute Proceedings,* Vol. 102 (March 1976). J. B. Mansfield (ed.), *History of the Great Lakes* (Chicago: J. H. Beers & Co., 1899). T. Michael O'Brien, *Guardians of the Eighth Sea: A History of the Coast Guard on the Great Lakes* (Washington: Government Printing Office, 1976). T. Michael O'Brien and Dennis L. Noble, "Heroes on Ninety-three Cents a Day," *IS* Vol. 33 (1977).

Information on the Northwestern University crew is drawn from material in the university archives, including a paper by Dean James Alton James, "Northwestern U.S. Life Saving Crews." See also O'Brien and Noble, "Heroes." The basic story of the *Calumet* rescue is in the *ARUSLSS, 1889*; it is reprinted in *IS* Vol. 30 (1974), as "Thanksgiving Day on Lake Michigan 1889; the Wreck of the Steamer *Calumet*." For background on Captain Cleary's test of a motor lifeboat, see O'Brien, *Guardians*, and Ernest H. Rankin, Sr., "Captain Henry J. Cleary, Lifesaver-Showman," *IS* Vol. 33 (1977). Details of the *Johnson* rescue are found in Dennis L. Noble, "Man the Surfboat!" *IS* Vol. 31 (1975), which reprints material from the USNA Records of the Coast Guard, RG 26. The loss of the Point aux Barques crew is described in "They Are All Gone," *U.S. Naval Institute Proceedings*, Vol. 102 (March 1976); in *ARUSLSS, 1880*; and in Mansfield, *History*.

For background on the *Waubuno* story see James P. Barry, *Georgian Bay: The Sixth Great Lake* (Toronto: Clarke, Irwin & Company Limited, revised edition, 1978); Dwight Boyer, *Ghost Ships of the Great Lakes* (New York: Dodd, Mead & Company, 1968); Fleetwood K. McKean, "The Wreck of the S.S. *Waubuno*," *IS* Vol. 21 (1965); and Teddy Remick, "The Finding of the Vanished *Waubuno*," *IS* Vol. 16 (1960). It may be of interest that Captain O'Donnell was my great uncle.

More on the *Alpena* loss is given in Boyer, *Ghost Ships* and in James L. Elliott, *Red Stacks Over the Horizon* (Grand Rapids; William B. Ferdmans Publishing Company, 1967). For the six ships lost on Lake Superior within 12 months, see Dr. Julius F. Wolff, Jr., "They Sailed Away on Lake Superior," *IS* Vol. 29 (1973), and the same author, "A Lake Superior Lifesaver Reminisces." For the loss of the *Anna C. Minch* see Dwight Boyer, *Strange Adventures of the Great Lakes* (New York: Dodd, Mead & Company, 1974).

Chapter 2

ALGOMA. I am indebted to Edith Gvora of the Thunder Bay Public Library for copies of news stories about the wreck. The most complete accounts are in the Port Arthur *Daily Sentinel,* Nov. 10 and 14, 1885. The quotations are from the former issue, which also prints the Marine Protest—the official report—filed by the officers of the ship. The registration record of the *Algoma* is in PAC, Shipping Register, Port of Montreal, RG 42, Vol. 410, Reel C-2469. Other records are missing at PAC. The 1885 *Annual Report* of the Ministry of Marine and Fisheries contains a brief account of the wreck and the findings of the investigation. The best secondary account is Fred Landon, "Disaster on Isle Royale," *IS* Vol. 21 (1965).

Acounts of the "last spike"—omitting the anecdote of the bent spike—appear in the Fort William *Daily Herald,* Nov. 9, 10, 11 and 14, and the Port Arthur *Daily Sentinel* Nov. 11, 1885. None of them makes the obvious, to us, contrast between the C.P.R.'s success on land and disaster afloat—perhaps a comparison that a true Victorian would resist. The story of the twisted spike appears in W. G. Hardy, *From Sea Unto Sea* (Garden City, N.Y.: Doubleday & Co., 1960) and other histories.

One discrepancy in the story of the *Algoma* wreck concerns the number of people lost. All reports I have found, with one exception, put the figure at 45. The only official document now available, the 1885 *Annual Report,* gives 38. Documentation for the latter publication is not now to be found, but as the other reports list the names of all 45 people, that figure seems the probable one. An apparent discrepancy is the location of the wreck on Greenstone Island; but that island is today called Mott Island and present-day Greenstone is farther along Isle Royale (see discussion in Port Arthur *News-Chronicle,* June 23, 1934).

The photographer's name is not in any contemporary report I have found. Landon gives it as J. F. Cooke. The 1934 *News-Chronicle* article lists A. Beggam, a photographer, and his assistant Walter Bailey as being among those on one of the tugs that went out to the wreck to recover bodies and property. Several tugs went at different times and it is quite possible that there was more than one photographer. Time certainly elapsed between the photo of the wreck still with sail and the one of it without a sail and covered with snow.

MONARCH. This account, in slightly different form, appeared in *IS* Vol. 36 (1980), as "The Wreck of the Steamer *Monarch.*" It is used here with the kind permission of the Great Lakes Historical Society. The article contains detailed footnotes.

Material on the wreck of the *Monarch* is in PAC, RG 42, Vol. 155, File 27884 and Vol. 158, File 27980. The registration record of the ship is at the Collector of Customs, Port of Sarnia. Reports concerning the wreck (for which I am again indebted to Edith Gvora) appeared in the Port Arthur *Daily News,* Dec. 10, 11, 12 and 13, 1906 and July 3, 1907; and in the Fort William *Daily Times Journal,* Dec. 11, 1906. There were also accounts in the Toronto *Daily Star,* Dec. 10, 1906; in the Toronto *World,* Dec. 11 and 12, 1906; and in the Sarnia *Weekly Observer,* Dec. 14, 1906. Later stories retelling the events of the wreck are W. Russell Brown, "Wreck of the *Monarch,*" Port Arthur *News-Chronicle,* June 3, 1944; and Jack Snider, "Below-Zero December Day when *Monarch* Foundered," Port Arthur Times-*Journal,* Dec. 18, 1961. A contemporary report, reprinting one of the accounts in PAC, appeared in *MR* Dec. 27, 1906. No record of the

rescue by the assistant lightkeeper or of his name has been found in USNA. Particular thanks are due W.A.W. Catinus, Chief, Marine Casualty Investigations, Transport Canada, who released some of the official documents.

The name of the photographer does not appear in any contemporary sources I have found, but is given in the secondary account by Jack Snider; John Skinner was definitely a member of the crew and so there is no reason to doubt the statement.

Those skeptical about compasses freezing should note the account of the *Altadoc* wreck 21 years later on Lake Superior, and the official record that a U. S. Coast Guard cutter that set out to help had to turn back because her compass froze.

GUNILDA. Boyer, *Strange Adventures.* Cleveland *Plain Dealer,* Aug. 31, 1911. *MR,* October 1911.

Several divers have tried to reach the *Gunilda* wreck over the years and some came close enough to see it. One, Charles King Hague, was killed in a 1970 attempt. In September 1980 the 140-foot oceanographic research vessel *Calypso,* owned by Jacques Cousteau, the French explorer, visited the wreck and sent down divers who reported that the yacht was in good condition, with the masts still standing and the rigging largely intact. One of the divers said, "If it's not the most beautiful ship we've seen under water, it is one of the most beautiful." (*New York Times,* September 21, 1980; *LLC,* October 4, 1980; *Detroit Marine Historian,* October 1980.)

Chapter 3

ROBERT WALLACE and DAVID WALLACE. ARUSLSS, 1887. Captain Adrian L. Lonsdale, "Rescue in '86," *IS* Vol. 30 (1974). Frederick Stonehouse, *Marquette Shipwrecks* (Marquette: Harboredge Press, 1974). Dr. Julius F. Wolff, Jr., "One Hundred Years of Rescues: The Coast Guard on Lake Superior," *IS* Vol. 31 (1975).

FLORA EMMA and ELIZA J. REDFORD. Through the kindness of Richard F. Palmer, I have obtained much of the information about these wrecks. Captain Anderson's account of the *Flora Emma/Redford* wreck, drawn from the Oswego *Daily Palladium* of Nov. 16, 1893, was provided by Mr. Palmer. (The quotations from Captain Fox and Engineer Connell are taken from the Palmer article, cited below.) He has discussed the wrecks at length in correspondence. The short quotations are from William Harrigan, a seaman on the schooner *Garibaldi,* whose account is given by Snider, cited below.

J. Leo Finn, *Old Shipping Days in Oswego* (Oswego: The Oswego County Board of Supervisors, n.d.). Richard F. Palmer, "Oswego in the Age of Tugboats," *T* Vol. 29 (1980). C.H.J. Snider, "Schooner Days," Toronto *Evening Telegram,* Aug. 21 and 28, 1937.

BALTIC and DANIEL G. FORT. Once again Richard F. Palmer has provided reference material: The Syracuse, N.Y., *Daily Standard,* Nov. 26 and 28, 1894. See also J. Leo Finn, *Old Shipping Days.*

SEVONA. Robert J. MacDonald (grandson of Captain McDonald) graciously provided information about the ship and the wreck and discussed the event in lengthy correspondence.

Other references are Boyer, *True Tales; Bayfield County Press,* June 28, 1956 (reprinting items from issues of Sept. 1905); ARUSLSS, 1906; and Certificates of Enrollment, *Sevona,* USNA RG 41.

MATAAFA. ARUSLSS, 1906. Duluth *Evening Herald*. Nov. 28, 29 and 30, 1905. "Wreck Report of the Steamer *Mataafa*," Nov. 28, 1905; "Investigation Report of the Steamer *Mataafa*," Dec. 14, 1905, both in USNA, RG 26, Records of the USCG, LSS. Dr. Julius F. Wolff, Jr., "The Shipwrecks of Lake Superior, 1900-1909," *IS* Vol. 27 (1971).

The *Mataafa* was salvaged and rebuilt, and she sailed until 1965, when she was scrapped at Hamburg, Germany (see *The Detroit Marine Historian*, March 1976).

LAFAYETTE and MANILLA. David Balfour, letter to the editor, *IS* Vol. 35 (1979). W. H. Law, "Capt. Wright's Story of the Lafayette," *IS* Vol. 13 (1957). *MR*, Nov. 30, 1905, Wolff, "Shipwrecks."

CYPRUS. ARUSLSS, 1908 (includes letters from Charles G. Pitz and Pickands Mather). *MR* Oct. 17, 1907 (includes account by Pitz). Wolff, "A Lake Superior Lifesaver Reminisces."

Chapter 4

Background on the Calvin fleet is given in D. D. Calvin, *A Saga of the St. Lawrence* (Toronto: The Ryerson Press, 1945) and in T. R. Glover and D. D. Calvin, *A Corner of Empire: The Old Ontario Strand* (Toronto: The Macmillan Company of Canada 1937). Both of the quotations given are from the latter book. The history of the Great Lakes Towing Company and wrecking in general has been covered by Alexander C. Meakin in two articles, "Commercial Wrecking on the Great Lakes," *IS* Vol. 24 (1968), and "Four Long and One Short: A History of the Great Lakes Towing Company," *IS* Vol. 30 (1974), Vol. 32 (1976), and Vol. 33 (1977). Barry, *Ships of the Great Lakes* tells of the *Eastland* disaster in detail, with photographs. Elue, Steven D., "The Wreck of the *Muskegon*," *T* Vol. 26 (1977), tells of that disaster; see also Elliott, *Red Stacks*.

Chapter 5

Navigational background is from O'Brien, *Guardians of the Eighth Sea*.

CITY OF BANGOR. "Report of Casualty, *City of Bangor*, Wreck Reports Received by the USCG," No. 795, FY 1927, RG 26, USNA. Consolidated Certificate of Enrollment and License, *City of Bangor*, RG 41, USNA. Dwight Boyer, *Ships and Men of the Great Lakes* (New York: Dodd, Mead & Co., 1977). Bowen, *Shipwrecks*.

ALTADOC. "Reports of Assistance Rendered by Eagle Harbor & USCGC *Crawford*, 8-11 Dec. 1927." Log of Eagle Harbor CG Station, Dec. 8-12, 1927. Log of USCGC *Crawford*, Dec. 8-11, 1927. Correspondence relating to assistance rendered by Eagle Harbor and USCGC *Crawford*. All, RG 26, USNA. Secondary accounts are in Bowen, *Shipwrecks*, and Dr. Julius F. Wolfe, Jr., "Canadian Shipwrecks on Lake Superior," *IS* Vol. 34 (1978). The "Correspondence" cited above points out that newspaper reports of the *Altadoc* wreck and rescue were not correct.

T.S. CHRISTIE. Report of Investigation of the Wreck of the *T.S. Christie*, with associated documents, USNA, RG 41, File 3391. Report of Casualty, USCG, *T.S. Christie*, USNA, RG 26, "Wreck Reports Received by the USCG," No. 238, FY 1934. *Manistee News*, Nov. 9, 1933.

HENRY CORT. Boyer, *Strange Adventures*. *Muskegon Chronicle*, Dec. 1, 3 (regular & extra editions), 5, and 26, 1934.

Chapter 6

For information about the St. Lawrence canals see Eric Schenker, Harold M. Mayer, and Harry C. Brockel, *The Great Lakes Transportation System* (Madison, Wis.: The University of Wisconsin Sea Grant College Program, 1976).

MILVERTON. I am in debt to Robert Graham for providing extensive references on the *Milverton* disaster. They include news stories of the day in the Massena *Observer*, Watertown *Daily News*, and Syracuse *Post Standard*, and information obtained from Capt. L. E. McDonald of St. Lambert, Quebec, and Daniel C. McCormick of Massena.

JOHN H. PRICE. Again I am indebted to Robert Graham, who very kindly provided a copy of the Report of Survey on the *Price*, newspaper clippings from the Hall Corporation files, and information on her salvaging drawn from the files of the various companies involved. He was familiar with the vessel after her repairs and knew her master from 1957-59, Capt. L. E. McDonald.

In addition, Mr. Graham has written about the wreck and subsequent career of the *Price* in "Hurt But Not Slain," *T* Vol. 29 (1980). Further information is in Ivan S. Brookes, *The Lower St. Lawrence* (Cleveland: Freshwater Press, 1974) and in Daniel C. McCormick, *The Wishbone Fleet* (Massena, N.Y.: privately published, 1972). Hugh MacLennan's comment is in his *Seven Rivers of Canada* (Toronto: Macmillan of Canada, 1961).

HENRY STEINBRENNER. USCG, "Marine Board of Investigation, Foundering of the S.S. *Henry Steinbrenner*," July 10, 1953, Washington, D.C.

NORDMEER. USCG, "Report of Investigation of M/V *Nordmeer* stranding on Thunder Bay Island Shoal, Lake Huron, on 19 November 1966," April 18, 1967. The quotation from Joseph Conrad is from *The Mirror of the Sea*.

PARKER EVANS and SIDNEY E. SMITH, JR. USCG, "Investigation into the Collision of the S.S. *Parker Evans* and S.S. *Sidney E. Smith, Jr.*, on 5 June 1972," Aug. 1, 1972. Laurence H. Lucker, Jr., "Let's Get Technical!" *T* Vol. 23 (1974).

ROLWI. USCG, "Report of Investigation of Collision of M/V *Rolwi* and S.S. *Marathonian* on 2 October 1973," July 2, 1974.

EDMUND FITZGERALD. Previous references to the wreck for Chapter 1, plus the following: *LLC*, Apr. 29, 1978 and May 20, 1978. Robert E. Lee, *Edmund Fitzgerald 1957-1975* (Detroit: Great Lakes Maritime Institute, 1977). Frederick Stonehouse, *The Wreck of the Edmund Fitzgerald* (Au Train, Mich.: Avery Color Studios, 1977). USCG, "Marine Casualty Report, S.S. *Edmund Fitzgerald*," Washington, D.C., July 26, 1977. USCG, "Summary of Results of Survey of Wreckage of *Edmund Fitzgerald*," Washington, D.C., n.d. Dr. Julius F. Wolff, Jr., "In Retrospect," *IS* Vol. 32 (1976).

In September 1980, divers from Jacques Cousteau's research vessel *Calypso*, operating a manned under-water vehicle, filmed the wreckage of the *Fitzgerald*. Jean-Michael Cousteau, son of Jacques Cousteau and supervisor of the diving and filming, afterward commented that damage to the freighter's starboard bow had obliterated part of her name, and that 100 feet of her midsection were missing. He speculated that the bow may have been damaged by striking the separated hull section and that that damage, plus the disappearance of the hull section, could indicate she had broken in two on the surface before sinking. (*Detroit Marine Historian*, October 1980).

PHOTINIA. In a personal interview, April 21, 1980, Lieutenant Commander Dennis Robbins very kindly explained the helicopter rescue.

Marine News (England), Vol. 34 (Feb. 1980). *Milwaukee Journal*, May 14, 1978. *Milwaukee Sentinel*, May 15, 1978. LLC, Dec. 8, 1979 & Dec. 22, 1979. USCG, "M/V *Photinia*, Grounding on 13 May 1978 with No Loss of Life," Feb. 9, 1979.

Chapter 7

Bowen, *Shipwrecks*. Dr. Julius F. Wolff, Jr., "One Hundred Years of Rescues: The Coast Guard on Lake Superior," *IS* Vol. 32 (1976).

Canallers not only had to thread their way through the tricky river currents of the St. Lawrence, but once in the lower St. Lawrence River or on the Gulf of St. Lawrence, they had to navigate some of the more difficult and wreck-strewn shores of North America. One such vessel, the 224-foot steamer *A. D. MacTier*, built in Detroit in 1913, weathered deep-sea service for the U. S. Shipping Board in 1918 and 1919. Back with her owners, the George Hall Company, on October 26, 1926, while carrying coal from Lorain, Ohio, to Chandler, Quebec, she grounded and then broke up in a storm off Cap d'Espoir, near the tip of the Gaspé Peninsula. (Courtesy Collingworth Museum)

Index

L

Lady Elgin, 9–10
Lafayette, 56–58
Lake Carriers' Association, 104
Lake Erie, 21, 62, 80, 83, 88, 89, 93
Lake Huron, 4, 5, 6, 8, 9, 16, 28, 64, 91–92, 93
Lake Michigan, 7, 9, 10, 11, 13, 15, 19, 22, 24, 25, 78–79, 80
Lake Ontario, vi, 3, 12, 21, 43, 61, 83

Lake Shore Engine Works, 13
Lake Superior, vii, 5, 8, 22, 23, 28, 31, 38, 42, 48, 51, 56, 58, 61, 68, 71, 74, 88–90, 101, 103, 109
Laura Grace, 36
Lawson, Lawrence O., Captain, 10
L. C. Smith, vii
Leafield, 22
Lefebvre, Alcide, Captain, 86–87

Len Higby, 11
Life Saving Service, U.S. *See* U.S. Life Saving Service.
Lochead, R. M., 32
Lucille Island, 68
Ludington, Michigan, 12, 13, 16, 24, 25
Lumby, John, 37

M

Mackin, William J., Captain, 72–73
Mackinaw, 93
MacLennan, Hugh, 85
Magna, 59
Magnettawan, 16, 18–19
Manila, 56–57
Manistee, 23, 79–80
Manitowoc, Wisconsin, 18
Maplehurst, 109
Marathonian, 98, 101
Marine and Fisheries, Department of, in Ottawa, 37
Mariners' Church, 8
Marquette, Michigan, 13, 41, 42–43

Massachusetts Institute of Technology, 13
Mataafa, 51–56
Maytham, 73
McBrier, James, 48
McCallum, Jack, 33–34, 37
McCormick, Rae, 34, 35
McDonald, Donald Sutherland, Captain, 49–51
McGarvey Shoal, 39
McGowan, J. L., 91–92
McLellan, C. H., Lieutenant, 13
McMaster, Captain, 36
McSorley, Ernest, Captain, 102

Melville, Herman, v
Milverton, 84–85
Misener, Scott, Captain, 24
Moby Dick, v
Monarch, 31–38
Montrose, 100
Moore, John, Captain, 28–31
Mooring, George, 37
Moose Point, 19
Muskegon, Michigan, 69, 80–81
Muskegon, 22, 67–69
Myra, 2

N

Naugatuck, 103
Navy Salvage Group, 95
Navy, U.S., 10

Nipigon Bay, 38
Northern Navigation Company, 36–37
Nordmeer, 91–93

Northwestern University, 9–10, 14, 16
Notices to Mariners, 71
Novadoc, 25

O

Ocha, Albert, 42, 43, 59
O'Donnell, John, Captain, 16, 18
Olympic Pearl, 98

Onassis, Aristotle, 98
Ontario, 3
Orient Trader, 100

Oswego, New York, 21, 43–48
Owen, James, Captain, 22–23
Owen Sound, Ontario, 28

P

Parker and Swain Wrecking Company, 62
Parker Evans, 93–94
Parry Sound, 16, 19
Parsons, John S., 46
Passage Island, 31–32, 34–36, 37–38

Peabody, C. H., Professor, 13
Pentwater, Michigan, 24
Pere Marquette, 3, 7, 13
Phillipie, William, 49–50
Phillipie, William, Mrs., 48
Photinia, 104–7

Pilgrim, iv
Pillsbury, 80
Pitz, Charles G., 59
Point aux Barques, 16
Point Traverse, 12
Portage Ship Canal, 42

W